AN ACCOUNT

OF

THE MANUFACTURE

OF THE

BLACK TEA,

AS

NOW PRACTISED AT SUDDEYA

IN

UPPER ASSAM,

BY THE CHINAMEN SENT THITHER FOR THAT PURPOSE.

WITH

SOME OBSERVATIONS ON THE CULTURE OF THE PLANT

IN CHINA,

AND ITS GROWTH IN ASSAM.

By C. A. BRUCE,
Superintendant of Tea Culture.

CALCUTTA:

G. H. HUTTMANN, BENGAL MILITARY ORPHAN PRESS.

1838.

AN ACCOUNT

OF

THE MANUFACTURE

OF THE

BLACK TEA,

AS

NOW PRACTISED AT SUDDEYA

IN

UPPER ASSAM,

BY THE CHINAMEN SENT THITHER FOR THAT PURPOSE.

WITH

SOME OBSERVATIONS ON THE CULTURE OF THE PLANT

IN CHINA,

AND ITS GROWTH IN ASSAM.

By C. A. BRUCE,
Superintendent of Tea Culture.

CALCUTTA:

G. H. HUTTMANN, BENGAL MILITARY ORPHAN PRESS.

1838.

life in a CUPPA
Chai Conversations

KAKOLI G

Published by
Renu Kaul Verma
Vitasta Publishing Pvt Ltd
2/15, Ansari Road, Daryaganj
New Delhi - 110 002
info@vitastapublishing.com

ISBN 978-93-90961-45-0

© Kakali Dutta
First Edition 2022
MRP ₹ 1295

All Rights Reserved.

No part of this publication may be reproduced, stored in a retrieval system or transmitted in any form, or by any means—electronic, mechanical, photocopying, recording or otherwise—without the prior permission of the publisher.

Editor: Papri Sri Raman
Layout and Cover Design: Somesh Kumar Mishra

Printed at Thomson Press (India) Ltd, New Delhi

Dedicated to the millions of
tea plantation workers, toiling
tirelessly with Meraki to source
the mystical brew

CONTENTS

VII PUBLISHER'S NOTE

XI FOREWORD

XV LOVE AFFAIR WITH TEA

01 Tea And Life

07 Not All Filmmakers' Cup Of Tea!

17 Future In A Cuppa...

21 Welcome To The World Of Specialty Teas

43 This majestic Samovar

47 Unfolding The Chai Story Of India

59 The Cup of Good Health

65 Tea Pairing

71 The Role Of Tea In The Indian Economy

79 The Importance Of Being A Tea Taster

87 The Ghost Of Namdang Factory Bungalow

99 Of Tea Tales

103 Let's Turn The Clock Back

131 Gratitude

Publisher's Note

Yes, we bring you a book on TEA. Many will think, yet another book on tea? Tea-lovers will say, the more the merrier. We say, it's a book like no other.

Your teapot lovingly pours out a miracle broth first thing in the morning, come rain or sunshine — a perfect beginning to a good day. And there still remains a last cup of comfort even if the day has been bad. Good times or bad, tea is a common sip today in every Indian household and workplace across the length and breadth of the subcontinent. Now it sits on your teapoy.

Life in a Cuppa tells the story of an extraordinary drink. It is not a book about just tea, it is a tale of transformation from the common to an uncommon concoction; in first-hand accounts, Piyush Pande and Suhel Seth talk of its personal and pop culture; others recollect ghost bungalows in distant estates and turn the clock back by sharing a 182 years old diary's pages on how to make tea.

The Author and Curator of this extraordinary book, Kakoli G, is an ardent tea enthusiast. Having travelled to far flung tea plantations across the country, she certainly has an edge when it comes to knowing her brew.

This book tells you all about the Steeping and the Sipping, Tasseography and Tasting, Pruning and Pairing and of distant dales with azure skies over rolling hills that produce 1,340 million kilogrammes of a variety of teas. The total turnover of the Indian tea industry is estimated at around Rs 10,000 crore, says CII chief Chandrajit Banerjee, emphasising India is the second largest tea producer in the world. More reason to have a book on tea.

One has rainbow recipe books on raitas and pakodas and salads and chutneys today; this perhaps is the first of a kind of recipe collection of teas — their exclusive recipes shared by none other than Alyona and Sanjeev Kapoor and Teamonk. These makers of magic potions tell us of the punchy essence of exotic spices like ginger, cardamom and cinnamon and ice teas with lemongrass.

Cold winter mornings or monsoon evenings, a cup of this chai is unbeatable at all times. From blending to brewing and bonding, it is a book like no other — it is *the* book on tea that Vitasta is proud to bring to our readers.

Sanjay Khosla was President, developing Markets of Kraft Foods (now Mondelez International) from January 2007 to March 2013. Before joining Kraft Foods, Khosla implemented a bold programme (Paint the World Yellow with Lipton) as Chairman of the Global Category Board for Hindustan Unilever Beverages. He was earlier the Executive Director for the beverage business in HUL.

Foreword

Tea is a phenomenal social connector. The first time this really hit me was in my first job as a salesman with Hindustan Unilever Ltd. I was responsible for sales in the Jammu territorial region in Northern India. My job was to sell soaps and detergents from shop to shop. I went to around 35 shops a day. In many shops, my attempts to sell failed miserably. In fact, I was asked to go away sometimes which was not good for my confidence. However, in some shops I was asked to sit down and have a cup of tea. This was a good sign. This meant that there was an emotional connection and the possibility of a successful sale. It also moved away from a cold transaction. On a good day, I often had 10 cups of tea. The tea was very strong with plenty of milk and plenty of sugar. Looking back, I realise this was probably not very healthy given the amount of sugar that was in the tea. Having hot tea during the peak of summer was also an interesting contradiction. Tea kept you alert. It made you calm at the same time. It also filled your stomach, as very often there was no time for lunch.

I had no idea then that I would get so involved with tea. Many years later, I was asked to lead the Brooke Bond Lipton Tea business, initially in India and then globally. It was a fantastic learning experience.

I had no idea how rich and deep the traditions and heritage of tea were. Tea served as a great connector to bring the leaders of two warring companies, Brooke Bond and Lipton, together as these companies merged. Also, what fantastic businesses Brooke Bond and Lipton were, built over generations. I learnt about some amazing traditions and rituals, like tea tasting. Very quaint, but very effective. I had no idea about tea tasting. Indeed, I made a complete fool of myself during my first tea tasting. I had come from a different industry and had no idea what to expect. I was on my first visit to the Brooke Bond Lipton tea tasting facility in Kolkata. There were rows of people in a large hall. With a lot of spittoons. I saw them perform an elaborate ritual.

They did not drink the tea. They swirled it around the mouth and then spat it out. The experts were able to differentiate between different products. I thought that was pretty amazing. I was encouraged to taste. Despite my best effort not to, I swallowed the tea. It was very embarrassing. I did limit my tea tasting after that. Years later, when I was responsible for the global tea category for Unilever based in Holland, I started appreciating the truly international nature of tea. I began to learn that while tea is globally relevant, tastes in different countries vary widely. It also became apparent that very often, a copy and paste approach to spreading products across markets does not work. One had to copy, adapt and then paste.

As I travelled around the world, I started learning about local tastes, traditions and the amazing relationship consumers had with tea. I remember visiting hot tea shops in the Middle East, all painted yellow. They were beautifully branded by our Lipton team. Shops buzzed. Fun, community, and social connections came together.

Visiting beaches in Portugal, I noticed Lipton was available everywhere. Interestingly, France, which was essentially a coffee-drinking culture, became one of the most successful Lipton markets in the world. Visiting our tea plantations around the world was like visiting paradise. Away from everything. Alone with nature. I can never forget memories from a Global Unilever tea conference that we organised in Kericho, Kenya. Everyone was housed in tents in the fields. The bonding and the feel of community was amazing. Glued together by tea. The whole group of leaders from around the world came together as One Team, One Dream, One Plan.

I also got exposed to the different forms of tea

including ready to drink iced tea. This was a whole new world. It was apparent that to grow dramatically, we needed access to new distribution channels. The desire to make Lipton available in vending machines in Japan, for example, led to a successful joint venture with Suntory, which immediately gave Lipton access to 400,000 vending machines. This led later to doing a global joint venture between Lipton and Pepsi. This joint venture has done well over the years, even though it was fascinating learning, trying to get two totally disparate organisations to work together.

Tea has a great tradition, a great history and a fantastic future. It will continue to connect us, warm our friends and family, offer us comfort and keep us rooted in our cultures. Tea has a fantastic opportunity for growth, as you look at it's potential to take share from other beverages as well. Not only is it relatively good for you, but tea makes you alert, yet can calm you down. As a colleague from Lipton once said, there is great potential for tea to improve your share of throat and indeed, share of your bladder. This book will give you a glimpse into that expansive world of tea. It will allow you to delve deeper into the concepts surrounding this wonderful beverage. I am grateful to Kakoli G for the invitation to write this foreword. I first met Kakoli more than 20 years ago in Bangalore when her husband Amit and I worked together. It is fabulous to see how she has developed as an author. I am sure this book will bring lots of insight and enjoyment to all of you.

Love affair with tea

Today, as I set out to tell a tale of this magical potion, many may exclaim what is so extraordinary about this ordinary drink!

To all, who have picked up this book, I would say 'Join me in the journey as we unravel together the various facets of teas'. And why not? A simple cup of tea has often been the only spark needed to make an acquaintance, inaugurating a bond of friendship that could last a lifetime. Tea has always been the trigger to getting people to come together and share the bond of love over a cuppa.
Let's start from the very beginning.

As a young bride, one of my most cherished wedding gifts was a blue pottery tea set with my name on it. A daunting job was how to make that perfect cup of tea for my husband, a tea connoisseur.

This started my immersion in the exciting world of teas, its various hues, the additives and most importantly the steeping time and the preparation technique. Knowing how to choose the right tea is just the beginning. The success of preparing that superb cup of tea comes from the mood of the individual

preparing the tea and the process. As time passed by, this cup of magic potion became a part of me. Me, my morning musings, my cup of Darjeeling and the newspaper. It was mesmerising to watch this flow, the careful mingling of the leaves with water, imparting its essence, brewing the tea, the slow unfurling of the leaves in the hot water releasing its amber colour and infusing into the water resembled a mandala pattern. It evoked a feeling of calmness. Watching it engage in a cosmic dance in the water, the gurgling sound of being poured into my cup, the warmth of the cup held in my hand, inhaling the gentle aroma and finally the indulging in this golden brew of elixir. Is it the taste, the subtle flavours, exquisite aromas or the amazing health benefits that draws me to it?

For me, tea has become synonymous with life, rejuvenation and wellness. I savour it with all my senses and gratitude as I move to my quiet corner to sit with my 'tea'. This simple five-minute ritual sets the way for the day as I unclutter the thoughts in my head and focus on being present. Aha this breath-taking moment, what to say of it!
Meditative?

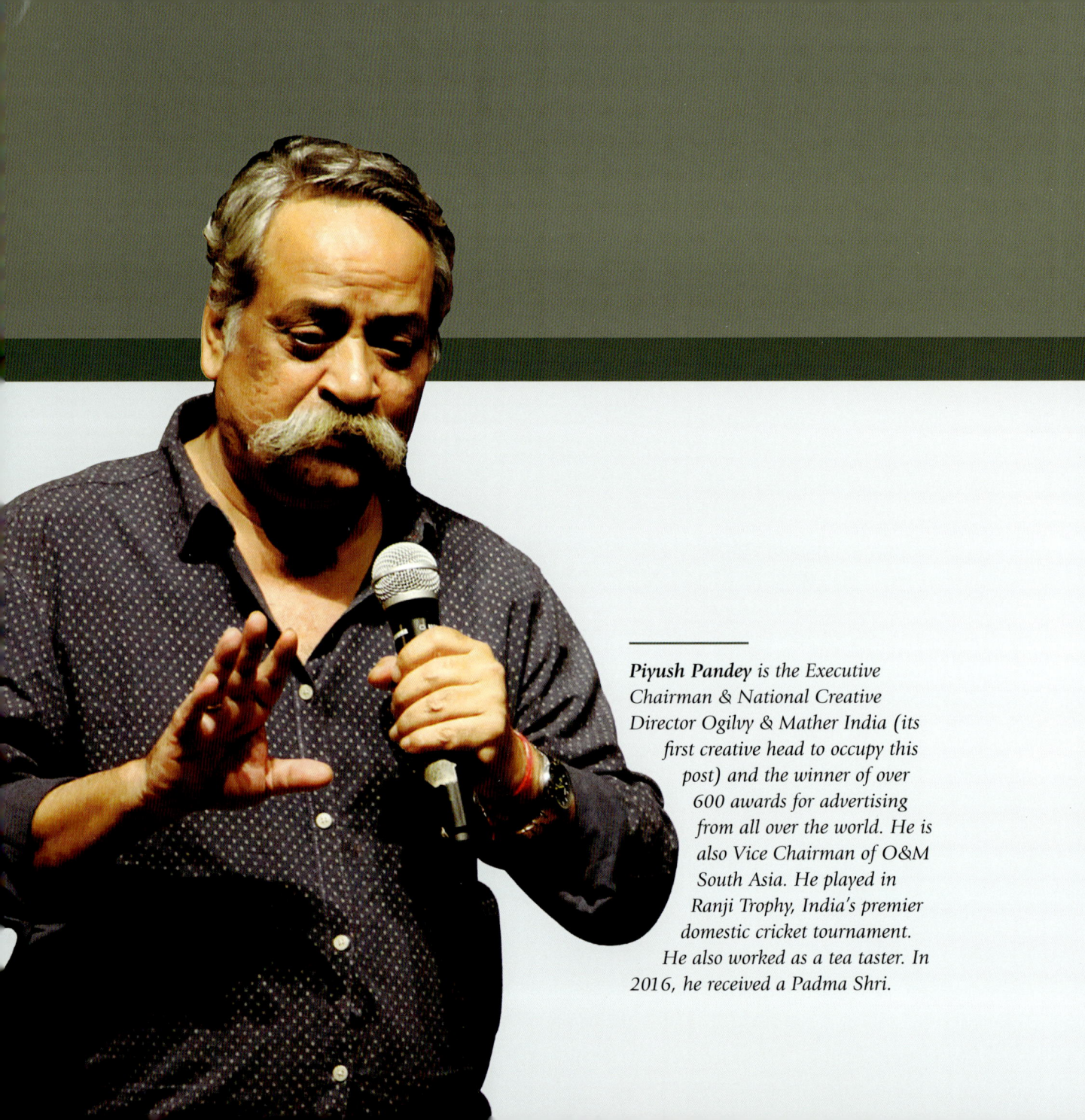

Piyush Pandey is the Executive Chairman & National Creative Director Ogilvy & Mather India (its first creative head to occupy this post) and the winner of over 600 awards for advertising from all over the world. He is also Vice Chairman of O&M South Asia. He played in Ranji Trophy, India's premier domestic cricket tournament. He also worked as a tea taster. In 2016, he received a Padma Shri.

Tea And **LIFE**

Chidiya choon choon karke boli bhor nikal ke aayee kya, bitiya padi bichhona pooche, 'Amma chai pakiyi kya?'

(Little birds are chirping as the sun rises/my little baby, tucked up in her bed, asks, 'Mother, is the tea cooked?').

This is my earliest memory of tea. On a freezing cold winter morning in Jaipur, when I was five years old, I woke up at five to a deep and melodious voice singing this verse. The voice belonged to my father, the target audience was my mother. The verse was created spontaneously, provoked by my sister asking my mother if tea was cooked. Cooked tea? Sounds strange? My father didn't correct my sister, going with the flow.

Tea is a special beverage in my life. It has many memories associated with it. It reminds me of Mom serving us tea when we woke up early in the morning to study for exams or to listen to commentary from Australia on radio. In college, it was about cutting classes and having 'chai' at Rohtas ka Dhaba in St Stephen's college. While playing Ranji trophy cricket, tea break was when the team gathered to discuss strategy for the last session of the day. In advertising, I started penning down ideas that brewed in my mind all night over a cup of tea served by my loyal

cook, the late Ghosto, at 7 am in the morning.

In office, tea was the beverage over which I met with fellow creative minds to crack an idea. When we got stuck, we ordered more cups of tea hoping it would break the deadlock.

It is 'omnipresent'. You can find dhabas and tapris wherever you go. You can get it in coffee shops — whether stand alone or in five star hotels and now there are chai bars. You can get it in crowded bylanes of India and on the highways in summers or in winters.

Enter a railway train and you can hear the strains of the tea vendor 'chai, chai, garam chai' (tea, tea, hot tea). Sit in an aircraft and every meal is rounded off with the question 'tea?'. It is always around.

It is 'omniscient'. It sees all kinds of people and hears all their stories. It is part of lives when people share their joys and sorrows.

Or when people churn their pains and challenges quietly within their minds. And so, it knows everything. 'Chai biskut' is start of the day for many daily wage labourers. It is a break for many factory workers. For people in offices it is a moment to congregate and 'gossip'. For the housewife, the 11 am cuppa is her 'me time'.

And in the afternoons, it is a part of her neighbourhood get-together. In the evening, it is the beverage for husbands and wives to spend time with each other, whether in conversation or quietly as the case could be.

It is 'omnipotent'. It can refresh, revive and relax and also stimulate — physically and mentally. As well as bond people. You drink tea to get up in the morning, and the evening cup is one over which people can relax.

In character, tea is much like Indians — a paradox of contradictions. As already mentioned, it can stimulate and relax — it all depends on what the mind wants it to do.

It is humble when served in khulads or as cutting chai.

It becomes special when served on silver trays and finely crafted cups and saucers. It is exotic when it takes the form of iced tea with fruits like peach and cranberry. It is a great unifier. For everyone in India, tea is a beverage.

Even in the South, mostly associated with coffee, tea is a staple during the day while coffee is the morning cup.

Yet, it is as diverse as India. The cup in the North is more 'badam (almond) coloured, sweet', while in the South it is more 'red' and 'bitter' in keeping with local taste preferences.

In physical form, it is more grainy in the Nnorth and dust in the South. Go East and they prefer the more aromatic teas from the foothills of Darjeeling. Most tea brands retailed in India have different blends for different States, to cater to local tastes.

It is healthy. It is natural because it is predominantly milk and tea. Most of the processing is done at home – no added flavours when it comes into the home in a pack. And with added spices like ginger and cardamom, it gets healthier. Yet, it is not healthy when it is had in excess – causing acidity. Sugar, even if it makes it more tasty, swings it to unhealthy.

In advertising stories, tea has been portrayed as both practical and inspirational — unique for any category in India. On one hand, it is about the 3 Rs (Revive, Refresh and Relax) and bonding, on the other, two iconic brands have used the beverage to tell more inspirational stories. Brooke Bond Red Label has used hospitality to break hostilities and social prejudices. Whether neighbours of different religious beliefs or social attitudes to sex workers, LGBT and most recently Covid patients, the brand stories have nudged society to look at people more open-mindedly. Tata tea has reawakened society by telling stories that ask for report cards of politicians and urging women to go out and vote. Clearly, there is something magical about tea in India. Though humble in composition, it has the power to actually move a billion Indians — physically, emotionally and mentally.

Though introduced to us by the British, I think, it has taken its own very Indian shape just like pizzas, burgers, noodles and pasta. Cooking tea? I said it sounded strange. But watch tea being made in India and you will realise that it is the Indian way of doing it. Water, tea, milk and sugar are all 'boiled' together before straining to make a hot cup of tea. Brewing is very English. We Indians boil-cook it. My sister was right – so that is why perhaps my father never corrected her.

Arnab Banerjee is a Film Critic who writes about Cinema. Besides being a film enthusiast, he also writes on music and arts. He writes for national dailies like The Times, The Asian Age and BBC.

Not All Filmmakers' Cup Of **TEA!**

In the 1981 Hindi film *Ek Duje Ke Liye*, starring Kamalahaasan and Rati Agnihotri as two lovers belonging to two different regions – Kamal a South Indian and Agnihotri a Punjabi – the parents of the two are perennially at daggers drawn due to their diametrically opposite views on virtually everything. In a scene where the bold and cheeky girl's mother catches her daughter's beloved's B&W photograph, and sets it on fire, the girl snatches the embers of the burnt picture and dunks them into her cup of tea and consumes it in a fit of defiant rage.

LIFE IN A CUPPA

While the scene is remembered for Agnihotri's fury, viewers cannot help but recall the storm that the tea cup entailed. In Basu Bhattacharya's film on marital discord, *Grihapravesh*, starring Sharmila Tagore and Sanjeev Kumar, the couple who are perpetually pinching pennies and trying to save for their own house someday, is shown consuming coffee every now and then.

That Kumar finds a new sexy girl Sarika at workplace as his love interest is not something that his wife would ever imagine. And when she does, what does she get to know about her? That her spouse's new love-interest loves drinking tea!

The story in which coffee is somewhat used as a metaphor to symbolise their conjugal bliss also suggestively denotes the drink as an aphrodisiac, wherein the other woman's tea drinking habit metaphorically serves as an impediment to their perceived perfect marriage!

Does tea feature as a remarkably spectacular presence in the story? In many European cinema, one has seen many conjoined dramatic moments with tea drinking activity while fewer examples are found in mainstream Hollywood. And, even lesser in our Indian films. There are a number of films where a vintage tea set or high-priced porcelain cups and saucers depict affluence more than anything else, and precisely nothing else. Stories in which more intense drama takes place around tea are mostly in the western world of cinema.

Jane Austen, whose oeuvre of only seven novels, a few plays, poems and stories, besides a novella, always revolves around women and their obsession to find a suitable match for themselves or their daughters, uses irony, humour and naked realism in her social commentary like few can match. While typically signifying the Victorian sentimentality, her principal characters often resort to long conversations over several rounds of tea. Of course, what they consume is less important than what transpires between them, but the beverage does become integral to the goings-on, save, perhaps in *Pride and Prejudice* where much discourse takes place over many rounds of tea.

Observant readers, rather viewers watching the film adaptation, would be amused at the idea of a cup and a saucer almost silently observing. Some may notice the consumption of tea as a mute participant of the loaded drama that takes place.

All of us would agree that drinking or serving tea with great company invites memorable instants of togetherness punctuated with unbridled laughter, and as characters iron out differences, the evening tea adds more heft in providing the right amount of camaraderie too.

It's rather natural to see many cold nations and some states in India where severe icy cold winds hit the winter months to experience tea drinking as a staple diet for almost the entire multitude. With good reason too. The piping hot brew always warms not just the mouth but the drinker also warms his hands while holding the cup. Hence, it's mostly an inclusive feeling of joie de vivre that lifts one's spirits that also prompts the consumer of the warm cuppa to open up and enjoy parleys to the fullest.

But, unless it is an alcoholic drink, beverages seldom play a significant role in any narrative of a movie. All that usually materialises or ensues in and around a narrative is the physical action or the choice of words spoken by characters. It is very rare to find the significance of any consumed or potable substance finding itself into the core of the engagement between characters.

But that's not all.

It is contrasted by many scenes of victuals or extravagant meals being prepared or ingested over lengthy dialogues. The instances can be seen in many regional language films, particularly in Bengali, Tamil, Marathi and also Hindi.

By the way, how many tea lovers who also happen to be passionate about cinema know that three of the most successful James Bond Stars, Daniel Craig, Pierce Brosnan, and Sean Connery have been self-confessed tea addicts? Grapevine has it that because of their addiction to tea, the actors often insisted on including a scene or two of them enjoying a cup or two, which most of the times was rejected by the directors only because it looked forcibly thrown in.

Come to think of it, the most common drink across all continents is, perhaps, tea in any form, be it the aromatic beverage in either freshly brewed or with a strong smell, or the most flavourful of teas, black teas, oxidised, green, red, white or oolong counterparts, its mildness or robustness is only incidental. Yet few writers have incorporated and blended its significance in popular fiction or on celluloid.

One of the hits in recent times, *Thappad*, the film starring Tapsee Pannu and Pavneet Gulati, has the female lead playing the subservient daughter-in-law who feels duty-bound to cater to the demands of her husband and his family. She obviously doesn't think much of her own dignity and feels obliged to engage herself with doing household chores as her be-all-and-end-all routine. Her plucking lemongrass from her home early morning to add that extra tinge and colour to the morning tea that she prepares so lovingly for her mother-in-law and her husband, adds to her being the quintessential perfect 'bahu' whose day must start with pleasing her marital family. The daily ritual of making tea for everyone typifies the expectations that every chauvinistic male in India has of his wife.

Moments in cinema are created with an interaction between characters, sometimes, silent communication too, and while an encounter results in a romantic liaison or a conflict or even a mundane conversational exchange, what they consume during their act is almost always secondary to the carryings-on.

However, that's more relevant to many Hollywood and European cinema.

When we look for moments with tea throughout, both the film adaptations of *Pride and Prejudice*, particularly when Elizabeth Bennet visits Rosings Park and must dine with the extravagant and superfluously esteemed Lady Catherine de Bourgh, one cannot ignore the elaborate arrangements that the table is adorned with. Yet again, one can only marvel at the writer's as also the film director's laying out the perfect setting for conversations to flow uninterruptedly over tea served in exquisite tableware that again connotes the overall well-being or the riches that the server of such a fine spread enjoys in society.

One would recall Austen's Emma, too, in which there are sequences with tea and picnics scattered throughout this romantic comedy. Most of her characters cement their ties while sharing tea at what is easily seen as a lavish setting.

In yet another instance where Tumnus in the Narnia books written by CS Lewis, primarily in *The Lion, the Witch and the Wardrobe* but also briefly in *The Horse and His Boy* and in *The Last Battle*, enjoy conversations with Mr and Mrs Beaver over a few warm cups of tea in some cozy scenes. The scenes are important as they help us understand what true courage is in the midst of chaos, emphasising the importance of continuing the journey together.

In the film, *The Lord of the Rings*, characters Gandalf, Frodo, and Bilbo, must share tea at the start of their big adventures, emphasising that subjects of great importance must be discussed over a warm brew. Author Tolkien is predominantly an advocate of the belief that the bonhomie enjoyed with close associates in any tight corner is best understood, enjoyed and celebrated over tea!

Besides magic and mischief, what also runs throughout the film adaptations of JK Rowling's Harry Potter series are candid moments with teacups and teapots, occupying an almost central thematic motif.

In the award winning film, *The King's Speech*, too, King George VI and his speech and language therapist Lionel Logue come from two diametrically opposite worlds but the analyst counsellor must earn respect from the Royal, not for any fancy titles or degrees but because of his proven merits. As mutual friendship and respect eventually bloom between these two men, they begin to share tea over long exchanges and discussions on various subjects.

LIFE IN A CUPPA

And tea assumes a legitimate and definite marker between their unusual bonding, as the King overcomes his stuttering and creates a lifelong friendship with Logue.

There have been other films, including Jahnu Barua's *Aparupa* and Kalpana Lajmi's *Ek Pal*, both set in Assam's tea plantations in which the storyline does centre around tea albeit more in terms of the backdrop than the context.

In *Mary Poppins* too, the iconic scene is a tea party in which three characters sit around a table and get lifted to the ceiling with their cups in their hands, a sure-fire shot that raises laughs but all because of them enjoying their tea. Also, in *Alice in Wonderland*, the Mad Hatter vehemently insists on Alice having a cup of tea with him only because he wants to meet her. There have been a few honourable mentions such as, *Earl Grey, Hot-Star Trek, The Great Gatsby* etc. where tea laid out on the table set the ball rolling for some thrilling encounters.

In India, two short films, *Cup of Tea* and *The Obituary* emphasise the importance of education and how relationships form an integral part of life. These two films succinctly convey some telling messages. But to watch a full-length feature with tea as a character (Well, almost!), is still not our filmmakers' cup of tea, this remains still wishful thinking!

Neera Sareen is an internationally acclaimed Master Trainer in Intuitive & Predictive Sciences, Tarot Master, Mentor & a Spiritual Transformation Coach. She has been studying Advaita Vedanta for some time at Rishikesh.

Neera is the founder of AUM KARMA – Centre for Holistic Studies , Meditation & Spirituality, New Delhi.

Future In A **CUPPA**...

Isn't it interesting to know what your stars have to say by merely sipping a hot cup o' Tea?

Read to know the new trend in fortune telling, alias Divination. Tasseography is an ancient art believed to have originated more than 5,000 years ago, beginning in China and spreading to Europe and Asia. It is an interesting technique, done through the patterns of tea leaves which appear in the cup and saucer after drinking it. It is referred to as a Symbolic representation of the tea leaves.

This technique is widely practiced in the Middle East, where it is a popular tradition passed down through generations. Since people first began drinking tea, they were fascinated by the shapes left in their tea cups, and this continues to be so today.

The accuracy of the Reading is immense, also depending on the practice, experience and depth of reading skills of the Tasseography Practitioner.

There is surely a process through which the whole reading is carried out. The time periods, phases of life, energy of occurrences and deep subconscious patterns can be studied with complete accuracy.

What is required is whole tea leaves, hot water, milk and sugar to prepare the tea. Assam, Darjeeling tea leaves are good to use and have calming aroma too. Tea leaves from Middle east is also good.

A plain set of cup and saucer is preferred to be able to read the images clearly. There are special cups available to do this, those that are less deep and have a wide mouth. The duration of an intense Tasseography session can last from 30 minutes to an hour.

If the seeker has anything in particular to ask then it's fine, else a general insight can also be given through a Reading.

The saucer image is equally important as it conveys a special message for the seeker, perhaps an instant action or a guidance.

It's also quite intriguing that the cup can at times reveal a pattern where there are three images joined together, for example animal head, human body and tail of a bird and these together give an information.

During one of my Tea Leaf Reading session, a person came to me and talked about a jewellery theft in his house and how his wife was being blamed for it.

The patterns formed in the cup and saucer which he drank from; amazingly the leaves spoke the truth.

The image of a dog appeared representing faithfulness. There was a scorpio and a lady representing hidden danger. The alphabet S appeared and an image of a child and head of a fox indicating a beginning of conspiracy. Sure enough, my observations came true. He came back to inform me that his brother's wife named Saroj was behind the theft and was conspiring against the family.

It was such an awe-inspiring moment for me and I feel gratitude to the universe and the Almighty who have bestowed enormous blessings on me for me to be able to read the past.

Kakoli G is the co-founder of a speciality tea venture, Teamonk. She likes to pen her thoughts on anything that catches her fancy. Be it tea, travel or tales from far-flung shores. A kaleidoscope of memories and learnings gleaned from her interactions with a large spectrum of society have found expression in her writings. She has authored two contemporary fiction novels, The Ambrosial Hour and Devi and the Enchantress.

Welcome To The World Of Specialty **TEAS**

Tea extraordinaire involving special processes from selection of tea bush, plucking of leaves to the process of converting tender tea leaves to the final brew – it's a tea trail worth following in small estates.

The clone of the tea bush is very different from normal tea clones and plucking is extremely delicate. Not always two leaves and a bud.

Sometimes just a bud or maybe a bud and a leaf.

Timing of plucking, exposure to withering, mechanised rolling, steaming and drying, all are managed under controlled temperature and humidity. The total quantity of tea produced in a day ranges from 30-50 kgs, compared to over 5,000 kg per day production in large tea factories.

From the land that gave the world Vedas and the saints, comes the finest of specialty tea collections curated by Teamonk.

This company has founders who are not only highly-qualified but also those who know how to source Teas – they know how to source and acquire the Best Teas – Orthodox, CTC, White, Oolong, Green, Puer and more.

Teamonk is a specialty tea venture, driven by a single-minded vision of offering the finest natural specialty teas to the tea lovers across the world. The completely integrated E-commerce platform enables the delivery of the handpicked, curated selection from the best tea plantations in India in record time worldwide.

It is said that a Buddhist monk was resting under a tree and accidentally a leaf fell into his drink making it taste delicious. In a moment of epiphany, he discovered Tea, much like Newton invented gravity! Only, more important. Buddhist monks have been drinking tea ever since to help them stay awake during long periods of meditation. But it is entirely possible, that tea also helps in a spiritual awakening of sorts.

But more times than not, this tranquil quality is lost somewhere in its journey from the gardens to your cup of tea. Like all good things, a good tea needs the utmost care and nurturing to bring out its best quality. And this is what Teamonk strives to bring to you.

Its teas are grown in beautiful pockets in the land of spirituality, India. The earth is organic and the air, pristine. The tea leaves are plucked at the precise moment of readiness by the loving and practiced hands of its tea pluckers. The leaves are processed with great precision by master artisans.

The processed tea is packaged by craftsmen whose only job is to keep its freshness intact. And this is the tea that is delivered to you in record time.

Kakoli G in conversation with **Ashok Mittal**, Managing Director, Teamonk.

Question: What is the difference between single garden teas, blended teas and artisanal teas? Any products in your portfolio which fall under any of these category?

Answer: Single garden teas are used as it is in the packaging without mixing with any other teas from other plantations. Blended teas are combination of teas from different tea plantations, and different regions. Artisanal teas are produced by small tea holdings who do not have tea processing facility and use largely hand rolling, kitchen facilities for drying etc.
Teamonk only uses single garden teas sourced through strategic alliance with the garden.

Q: A bit about specialty teas, please. And what is CTC?

A: Specialty teas are specially processed unlike conventional tea processing. The quality of tea bush, fine plucking standards, processed in small unit with steaming, rolling and instant drying to avoid oxidation. Also hand rolling/sun drying is involved to minimise use of machines.
CTC is cut tear curl, a traditional black tea consumed in India (about 90 per cent of Indian tea is CTC process tea). It is small, granular black tea produced by cutting the tea leaves into smaller pieces, granulating it through machine, oxidising for black tea characteristic — colour, strength — and dried, sorted for packing.

Q: If Darjeeling is said to produce the Champagne of teas, how would you describe Assam, Nilgiris and the Kangra teas? What is so unique about them?

A: Each region has its own characteristic based on soil, rainfall, sunshine, temperature etc. Assam teas are known for golden bright tea liquor, strong and pungent: Nilgiris is known for their black orthodox teas: Darjeeling teas for its exquisite flavour, strong aroma and coloury appearance. Kangra valley produces specialty teas in small manufacturing units — green, oolong, white etc which have a distinct characteristic and delicate flavour.

Q: Let's talk about the tea auctions. How does Teamonk procure its tea?

A: Tea auctions are meant to secure best price for the seller and ensure every buyer has access to the sample and has evaluated it before bidding. Nowadays auctions are held electronically, and buyer can buy online from anywhere. Teamonk doesn't buy in the auctions and all sourcing is direct from tea gardens through strategic alliances.

Q: Indonesia and Vietnam – how would you describe the 'way of tea' in these countries?

A: Internal consumption of tea in Indonesia is approximately 50 per cent of the total production and rest is exported. However, there is also some import of quality CTC black teas. Vietnam has increased its tea production from 25 million Kg/annum to nearly 150 million kilogrammes over last twenty years through sustained efforts, new cultivation and government support. Vietnam's tea quality is low medium, medium, primarily orthodox varieties. In Indonesia, tea production is similar to Vietnam and has not grown much in the last decade. Apart from black tea, Indonesia also produces they are significant quantity of green teas and is consumed as pure green as well as Jasmine green tea. Quality wise, black tea is primarily orthodox variety, give light coloury liquor and used as a filler by tea blenders from East Africa by major tea companies like Unilever for their export of branded teas like Lipton.

Q: Why Teamonk – its uniqueness, how did it manage to survive despite stiff competition or rather how did it ride on the popularity wave from inception in 2016 till date?

A: Teamonk is only focused on specialty teas, sourced from mountain regions of Darjeeling, Nilgiris and Kangra valley. We only use long leaf orthodox teas to ensure soothing taste with delicate flavour and all green teas are curated with natural ingredients like spices, herbs, fruits and flowers for taste and health. We have survived the stiff competition only on the strength of our expertise and experience and by ensuring finest quality of teas and ingredients for our tea connoisseurs and tea lovers. Teamonk contributes to a balanced score card approach – P&L, people and planet. It is very conscious of its responsibility as a professional organisation. Therefore, apart from ensuring health of the business, we pay remunerative prices to our suppliers, support tea plantation workers through scholarship for their children, we have a totally non-polluting business operation with virtually no carbon emission.

THE ART AND SCIENCE OF
BREWING

Tea is a highly exotic substance and to savour tea-time fully, one must know how to take time out to relax, leave daily worries behind and appreciate the simple pleasures of the moment.

Perhaps no other beverage has been the object of such sanctification and ceremony than tea has been.

The tea plant is a member of the Camellia family. Initially it was classified as Thea sinensis (sinensis means China) by Linnaeus in 1752. The description was based on a drawing by a gentleman called Kaempfer, of a plant found in Indonesia. Classifications were given to other Thea genera i.e. t.bohea, for black tea manufacture and t.viridis, for green tea manufacture. Finally, to put an end to all the confusion surrounding the name given to the tea plant, in 1935 at the International Botanical Congress, held in Amsterdam, it was decided to combine the two genera Thea and Camellia into a single genus Camellia. The widely accepted view today is that tea is made from three main types: Camellia sinensis, Camellia sinensis var. assamica (from Assam, in India) and Camellia cambodiensis (which has red tinged leaf, from Cambodia and neighbouring hill regions). Camellia irrawadiensis,

2nd leaf

4th leaf

Older leaf

considered a Burmese endemic is a true tea but contains no caffeine.

The Indian variety of tea was found by Major Robert Bruce in 1823 in the Patkoi Hills of Upper Assam and it was from here that the foundation of the Indian tea industry was laid.

The tea plant has dainty, scented white flowers, and has the ability to grow into a shrub of around 15 - 20 ft height. The young tender shoots are harvested for tea making, generally consisting of two leaves and a bud. For commercial reasons, the present-day industry recognises two forms of tea namely the small leaved China bush Camellia sinensis and the large leaved Assam (Camellia assamica). A third form is the Cambod or Southern Form considered to be a hybrid of the China and Assam varieties, and combines the qualities of both.

Brewing tea is an art and connoisseurs insist on being perfect to the 'T', to create this magical potion.

The teapot, the principal tool in the tea making process is to be treated with utmost care. It should never be washed or scrubbed with harsh chemicals, but left under running water, rinsed thoroughly and then allowed to dry in the open, uncovered. This helps to retain the deposit of tannin that layers the side of the tea pot slowly and enhances the flavour of the tea brewed in the pot.

1st leaf

3rd leaf

The quality of water used for brewing tea is as important as the process itself. It should be pristine, fresh, odourless and preferably free from calcium. An alternative is to use filtered water.

Water may be heated in a kettle. The sole purpose of the kettle should be limited to only warming water for tea- the water should just simmer and not boil to retain the flavour of the tea. Boiling makes the water flat and lifeless, it may harm the tea leaves and alter its flavour. This water should then be poured on the leaves placed in the warm teapot.

A thumb rule for the right amount of tea leaves to be used is approximately one teaspoon to a cup. Steeping is the act of letting the flavour of the tea infuse into the water and connoisseurs suggest a minimum of two minutes – too long a time causes the tea to become bitter.

The semi-fermented teas need a good 3 mins to bring out the best in them. Green tea requires maybe 2-3 mins for that ultimate flavour. White tea, which is the purest, least processed tea, air dried and only slightly oxidised, requires a steep time of 1-3 mins.

Pu-erh – the Bordeaux of tea – green Chinese tea that is fermented and aged before it is pressed into cakes requires a steep time of 1-3 mins. Tea is a fragile and precious commodity and must be stored in an airtight container away from dampness and light.

A general principle to be followed for the shelf life of black tea would be a year, and it is about half a year for semi-fermented and green tea.

For a true tea connoisseur, it is considered a sacrilege to employ additives like milk, sugar or lemon. Perhaps for morning tea, milk maybe added, but for green tea, semi fermented teas, lighter Darjeeling tea, milk is an absolute no-no. A highly debatable point though. Certain full-bodied black teas like those from Assam and Sri Lanka can do with a drop of milk, to mellow down the tannin content. A slice of lemon added to tea alters the flavour and hue and it is best avoided, though one may prefer to have it with ice-tea.

Adding sugar is up to individual taste and can be used in black tea.

Making ice-tea at home is fun, and a much healthier option in hot summers, than the coolers laden with sugar and preservatives. After brewing hot tea as normally done, it can be chilled in the refrigerator or simply poured in a glass filled with ice. Another way of making ice-tea is by combining equal number of tea bags and equal cups of cold water in a large pitcher.

It is then covered and chilled for at least four hours. Tea bags are discarded and this cold brew – iced tea, may be served with lemon slices according to one's personal taste.

The tea can be consumed straight or on ice, even mixed with ingredients to create exciting cocktails. While preparing a cup of tea seems a simple exercise, preparing any of the hundreds of teas available requires attention and knowledge.

Making a delicious cup of tea is a play of tea leaves, the amount of water used, water temperature, the time of infusion, and the vessel the tea is brewed in. Following the correct directions for a tea can make even an ordinary tea satisfying, while brewing a rare, expensive tea incorrectly can lead to a bitter, undrinkable infusion.

GREEN TEA vs GREEN COFFEE

Green embodies the colour of spring, a hue associated with life, rejuvenation and health.

It is of no surprise then, that the world is slowing turning to embrace green in a major way!!

Be it the 'morning cup to start afresh' or the midday 'pick me up cup', going green is the new mantra.

Green coffee or green tea?

As the cousins with the common name tag green battle it out to seek attention, the consumer's predicament is understandable.

Quite a difficult task to rank the benefits of these two beverages and declare one as a winner.

Coffee is basically the seeds of berries procured from the plants C arabica or C robusta.

Simply put, green coffee is the regular coffee beans that are unroasted and raw. These green coffee beans are cleaned before use; hence they retain their natural green tinge.

A cup of this green beverage will not taste like the regular coffee, in fact, this mild green liquid would taste more like a cup of herbal tea.

This pale-coloured brew is best enjoyed without milk or sugar just like green tea. It is said to boost one's metabolism, curb appetite, improve blood circulation and burn fat.

Yes, it does contain a high dose of antioxidants known as chlorogenic acids. In fact, as the coffee beans are not roasted, the compound retains its potent properties that benefit our body.

The best time to have green coffee is a couple of hours before mealtime. There are a few reasons for it.

Firstly, Chlorogenic acid present in green coffee reduces food cravings. This helps curb the desire to unnecessarily gorge over unhealthy food items.

It also affects the absorption of vital elements like folic acid and iron which could lead to a reduced haemoglobin level in the system.

Hence having green coffee after a full meal is best avoided.

Another harmful side effect of green coffee vis-a-vis green tea is the presence of excess caffeine.

Over-indulging in green coffee can cause symptoms like high blood pressure, anxiety, headache, upset stomach and insomnia.

Moderation is the key to benefit from this beverage; hence it is advisable to limit it to two cups in a day.

Tea, on the other hand, is obtained from the leaves and buds of the evergreen shrub Camellia sinensis.

Unlike black (completely oxidised), oolong (semi-oxidised), green tea is unfermented and has not undergone the withering and oxidation process.

These teas are processed mainly by pan-firing or steaming.

Green tea, loaded with antioxidants called catechins enhances metabolism, helps in clearing the system, improves immunity, helps lose weight and improves cardiovascular health by reducing high blood pressure.

The polyphenols in this magic potion help reduce stress, anxiety, depression.

Although not an excitant, this tea re-energises and re-invigorates the system. It also has a reputation of being an intellectual stimulant. It uplifts the mood and relaxes the mind.

Green tea and meditative practices are like two peas in a pod. Both of them have a calming effect, helps de-stress and relax.

The antimicrobial, antioxidant and anti-inflammatory effects promote oral and dental health by reducing the risk of periodontal ailments and dental caries.

Again, indulging in anything in excess can have an adverse effect on the system. So, it is a good idea to limit your green tea intake to four cups a day.

A personal favourite of mine is the Rose green tea from Teamonk… a striking combination of rose petals amidst pure green tea leaves sourced from the highlands of Nilgiris.

There is this dilemma I often face, when I pick up this aromatic cup of green tea. Is it the superior taste and subtle flavour or the amazing health benefits due to its rich antioxidant content which draws me to it?

For me this is what 'going green' really means… a sip of this exquisite tea with a fresh floral flavour.

An absolute bliss for my tastebuds.

As we delve into the topic of this magical shrub, realisation slowly sets in that to bracket off tea into a narrow segment as 'just another beverage' would be a costly mistake.

WU-LONG, OOLONG, THE BLACK DRAGON TEA

Each cup tells a thousand tales as it transports one to an imaginary world, gently nudging one to trudge along and visualise its origins.

It could be a harvest season in springtime on Himalayan ranges for the slightly astringent first flush black tea: hot summer in Ceylon for full bodied black tea: to the humid Formosa islands for that special semi-fermented oolong tea, maybe the impressive Japanese tea gardens in early May when the world's finest green teas are harvested or to the highlands of Kenya where purple tea is cultivated. As one criss-crosses between the world of strong malty black teas to delicately flavoured white teas to the grassy green teas or the floral oolong, the perception of tea changes. One slowly becomes conscious of the uniqueness of this plant. As we start exploring the world of this wonder shrub, interesting facts emerge. There are more varieties of tea in China than there are wines in France; that the flavour of Darjeeling teas changes as the seasons change; that there is not only a tea for every palate but for every moment of the day; that the tea leaf itself upholds the distinguishing characteristics of the soil which bore it and tells a thousand tales – that this magical brew is a cup of elixir overflowing with amazing health benefits. It is time to sit back, relax and listen to the mesmerising narrative of this peerless plant.

Tea contains a natural enzyme called a 'polyoxidase' enzyme. When the leaf is bruised, twisted or cut, it comes in contact with oxygen in the air. This chemical change causes the leaf to turn brown. At this stage, the leaf has a very pleasant, spicy, aroma – teamakers call it the 'fermentation nose'. It is fed straight into a drier at this juncture. To put it down simply, all teas come from the same plant Camellia sinensis. The difference lies in the procedures that is carried out after harvesting the leaves.

LIFE IN A CUPPA

BLACK TEA

Harvesting-Withering-Rolling-Fermentation-Drying-Sorting-to Blending and Packing.

OOLONG TEA

Harvesting-Withering-Rolling-partial Fermentation- Drying-Sorting-to Blending and Packing.

GREEN TEA

Harvesting-Withering-Sometimes un-withered fresh leaf- Steaming or Hot panning-Drying-Sorting-to Blending and Packing. An interesting fact to note is that fresh tea shoot contains about 75-77 per cent moisture but if these shoots are rolled, cut, or macerated they tend to turn into flat, open, flaky particles and this is when we witness floaters on the top of the cup. When about 5-10 per cent moisture is driven off the leaf, it has a wilted, flaccid appearance. When rolled, it turns into twisted wiry, solid particles of all shapes and sizes which, when dried, are attractive for the trader as well as the user.

WHY IS BLENDING REQUIRED?

Tea from any single plantation tastes different with each harvest, way of processing the leaves also impacts the flavour. At times, the tea from the same source can be fairly bland and tasteless, sometimes bitter and astringent and on many occasions can have an alluring aroma and unparalleled taste.

All this point in one direction. Packing tea from a single source and selling may not be the best idea always. Customers would be clueless as to why the tea tasted brilliant at one point and at times the infusion was undrinkable.

Customers demand consistency, a uniformity in the taste when they are purchasing teas.

The only way to achieve this is by having a coalition of teas with different characteristics, complimenting each other and resulting in a product, consistent in taste.

Taste differences are caused by a number of factors. Too much rain and prolonged overcast conditions can result in very thin liquoring teas with a bland taste. High temperatures will affect the growing tea and many of the compounds which make up the aroma of tea can be lost. Hours of sunlight, rainfall and even the time of year makes a difference.

The standard of the harvested leaf is of major importance and only the new two tender leaves and a bud should be harvested. Coarser long shoots will make an inferior tea. In Ceylon, 0-2,000 ft is classified as a LOW GROWN 2,000-4,000 ft is a MEDIUM GROWN and 4,000-6,000 ft and above, has a classification of HIGH GROWN. High grown tea is considered to be the best. Having said that, well, there are teas coming in from a place like Assam having a cool winter but no altitude, but are cherished. These teas have a unique malty flavour, the strength and colour in cup that are second to none. For the consumer, it all comes back to personal preference.

LET'S CATAGORISE
TEAS

Categories differ according to usage, place, tastes, smells and processes.

Specific Origin, that is the region where it comes from. India, Africa, Ceylon, Indonesia or wherever – they are all teas blended with others from the same region.

Specific Occasion ones go under many different names like Afternoon tea, Irish Breakfast, English Breakfast, and so on. They are all blended teas and can contain teas from a number of countries.

Specific Flavours are called Earl Grey which is flavoured with Bergamot or the Moroccan green tea with mint.

An unblended tea, called a 'Single Estate Tea' would come from a named plantation tea estate, for example, Okayti, Darjeeling. These are renowned plantations, acknowledged by many as being the best, the name thus becomes an indicator of a certain standard. A tag mentioning 'pure unblended Ceylon tea' or 'pure unblended Indian tea', so on and so forth on the tea packet, immediately brings to mind that this unblended tea is superior to a blended tea. This inference is not correct. A pure 'unblended Indian/Ceylon tea' could have a large number of teas going into the final product. Large producer countries have many plantations in different districts.

The teas are drawn at the auctions to blend together to give a bulked 'country of origin' tea. The four main types of tea are White, Green, Oolong, and Black Tea. The two main types of manufacture are: Orthodox, a gentle kneading and rolling process, and CTC, a severe

crushing, tearing and curling of the leaf between sharp toothed, stainless steel rollers.

One can only speculate as to how the first teas were made but it is most likely that the shoots of the tea bush were harvested, dried in the sun, and then prepared with boiling water. This would be near to what is called 'White Tea' today.

Oolong tea, as mentioned earlier, refers to a semi-oxidised type of tea in between the green (non-oxidised) and black tea (completely oxidised). Oolong tea has an unique taste and alluring aroma and is characterised by a reddish brown appearance. The leaves of the same plant (Camellia sinensis) is used to make black, oolong, green and white tea. The differentiating part is the process to prepare oolong tea. Here, the plant is withered under strong sun and then goes for oxidation before curling and twisting. The degree of oxidation ranges between 10 to 80 per cent, hence the flavours and taste also vary from being sweet floral, honeyed fruity, woody or grassy and vegetal. Smoother than black, less fresh and leafy than green, Oolong teas exhibit balance and harmony.

Well, most teas contain compounds that enhance weight loss naturally. However, research has revealed that the catechins compounds in green and oolong teas induce thermogenesis, that is the body's natural ability to turn fat into energy. This process helps the human body to lose all that unwanted fat.

There are many versions as to how this mystic oolong tea came to be known as the Black Dragon Tea. A popular version is about a hunter, nicknamed Black Dragon in the Fujian Province of China. While chasing a deer one day and trying to hunt it down, he forgot about his bundle of freshly plucked tea leaves in his bag. As time passed the leaves started to oxidise and the colour changed to almost brown. By the time the young man started processing this semi-oxidised tea as he did normally, a highly fragrant, flavoured tea emerged – quite distinct from the earlier ones he was used to.

Today, Taiwan is world famous for its aromatic high mountain oolongs. Here the oolong teas undergo a longer fermentation, almost sixty per cent and has a golden brew with more of an occidental flavour. This is a highly sought-after semi-fermented tea appreciated much by people who prefer light aromatic teas. Premium quality oolong tea can be steeped several times from the same leaves. It improves with rebrewing and this is one of the most amazing facts of oolong tea. Oolongs prepared in the Occidental way are generally steeped for 30 seconds to a minute and can be re-steeped 5 to 7 times, depending on the type of oolong.

Homemade iced tea using high quality tea is fortified with antioxidants and is simply delicious.

CITRUS OOLONG

A teaspoon of oolong tea is steeped in 1 cup of water for a minimum time of 5 minutes. The strained liquid is refrigerated until cold. Add fresh lime juice and enjoy the tangy twist. If you still carve for that sweetner, add honey. Bursting with antioxidants, this is an ideal thirst quencher during the summer months.

CINNAMON OOLONG ICED TEA

In 4 cups of hot water steep 4 tablespoons of oolong tea with 4 cinnamon sticks for about 5-7 minutes. This concentrated liquid is strained and refrigerated. Amount of cold water added to dilute it is according to personal taste and the tea may be served over ice.

Cinnamon is a wonder spice. It has anti-inflammatory properties, is a high source of antioxidants, protects dental health and freshens breathe naturally.

Oolong and green tea combination

An ideal weight loss recipe is to steep oolong and green tea (1 teaspoon each) in a cup of hot water for 5 minutes. The liquid is strained. Sip this invigorating refreshing drink slowly, to get rid of those love handles.

This tea drunk twice a day will ensure burning of excess fat. Both green tea and oolong tea have catechins which helps in weight loss and improve triglyceride levels in the human body.

Like with anything good in life, moderation being the key word, it is advisable not to drink more than two cups of oolong tea in a day. One cup in the morning and one cup in the afternoon is recommended for weight loss. They are low in theine and therefore can be considered as an evening beverage.

Picture Courtesy Kashmir Origin

This majestic SAMOVAR

Kakoli G

I fell in love, the moment I set my eyes on it! The Chinar motifs gleaming through the reddish tint ! The light peeping through the maze of crisscross metallic net at the bottom was bewitching! The curved pinnacle on the crown was striking. I slid my hand through the chain fixed between the spout and the handle and tried to lift it – ponderous.

This majestic Samovar in my living room has always been a conversation starter. Made of copper, weighing ten kilos, this traditional Kashmiri kettle is used to brew, boil and serve tea – the famed 'noon chai' and the 'Kashmiri kahwa'.

The samovar is believed to have originated in Russia. As Russia's cultural influence grew in the eighteenth century, the use of the Samovar for brewing teas spread to Eastern Europe, Iran, Afghanistan, Azerbaijan, Kashmir and the Middle East as well.

Roughly translated the Samovar means 'self-brewer'. People believed that samovars had a soul and could communicate with people based on the sounds produced while heating the water!

It was introduced in Kashmir via the age old trade routes in the medieval times. The highly creative, indigenous Kashmiri artisans worked on the Russian Samovar, remodelled and recreated the copperware, which today depicts the rich culture of the valley. Generally, Kashmiri samovars have calligraphic motifs engraved on them. Multiple artisans are involved in creating this heritage tea brewer. Indeed a collective effort put in by Khar – the smith, Naqash – the engraver, Zarcod – the gilder, Roshangar – the polisher and Charakgar – the cleaner or finisher. Inside the Samovar is a mini-world where the tea is brewed. It consists of a chamber of fire; a copper pipe with alloy buff runs vertically through the centre. This is home to burning coals which heats up the entire kettle from the inside.

Around the fire-container, there is a space for water to boil. Tea leaves, sugar, cardamom and cinnamon are put into the water for preparation of the beverage.

The main body is connected to the bottom of the Samovar by the 'Neck'. It contains holes for the descent of excess heat and for air circulation. The whole weight of the Samovar rests on the rounded bottom part.

There are two variants of Samovars used in Kashmir. The copper Samovar used by Muslims and that of Brass used by Kashmiri Pandits. A sentiment popular among the local people is that drinking tea, milk, or water from a Samovar has some therapeutic value that benefits health.

Words fall short while describing the grandiose of a Samovar.

It carves its own space, perched regally, as we sit around it on a cold winter evening sipping our favourite kahwa, seeking warmth and succour.

Celebrity **Chef Sanjeev Kapoor**, one of the most known faces of Indian Cuisine with a huge fan base across various Social Media platforms, was the host of the famous food show *Khana Khazana* that ran for 18 years on television. He now runs his TV Channel *Food Food* and is owner of the Khazana range of food products & Wonderchef – premium brand of kitchenware, cookware. He is also the winner of the prestigious Padma Shri award.

Unfolding The Chai Story Of **INDIA**

India, a country of mesmerising beauty, is not so just in terms of the rich culture and heritage but also because of the opulent and diverse cuisine it has to offer. Our rich gastronomic delights have left the most fastidious of the culinary experts spellbound by its flavours, textures, methods of preparation and exquisiteness. And in this intriguing country, there exists a love which is unexplainable, irreplaceable and knows no boundaries – the love for cha, chai or tea! Being the second largest tea producer in the world, you can find a *tapri* (dhaba) at every possible corner of a typical Indian street and a diehard lover of this evergreen beverage sipping on his cuppa of chai. A true blue desi might agree to the fact that there's no other beverage in the world that can even come as a close competitor to the beloved tea.

Chai is an emotion that has been a significant part, both in good and bad times, exam stress, hectic workdays, treating health issues, deep conversations about life and the likes. There is no end to this list to prove what a blessing it is, in all our lives. Like other dishes, India has a range of popular chai variations inspired by the local tastes specific to different regions. While we all might have our own special chai to soothe our taste buds every now and then, there is no harm in knowing more about the diverse tales of the extravagant tea palets from all over the Indian subcontinent. Tea lovers, there are many other tea variations waiting to be explored and this one's going to be a beau-tea-ful ride!

Dive deep into this beautiful world of popular regional tea versions of Bharat. Read on…

Pan-India

Masala Chai: Masala chai is the most popular tea that holds a very special place in the heart of every Indian. The aromatic flavour of tea is enhanced with the punchy essence of numerous desi spices like ginger, cardamom and cinnamon among others. Cold winter mornings or monsoon evenings, a cup of this chai is unbeatable at all times. Making the perfect cup of masala chai is no less than an art and if you want

to lace it, you should know the perfect breakdown of spices that goes into the process of making a cup of this lovely brew. My family love their evening cup of masala chai with garmagaram vada pav, studded with fun banters, especially during the monsoon season. So, here's my go to this good ol' beverage:

INGREDIENTS

½ tbsp tea leaves | 4 green cardamoms | 1 inch cinnamon | 1 black peppercorn | A pinch of fennel seeds (saunf) | 1 inch ginger, peeled | ½ cup milk | 1½ tbsps sugar

METHOD

In a mortar, add green cardamoms, cinnamon, black peppercorn, fennel seeds and crush to a coarse mixture with the pestle. Transfer on a small plate and set aside.

Add ginger in the same mortar and coarsely crush it. Set aside.

Boil 1½ cups water in a deep saucepan, add tea leaves, crushed spice mix and ginger, mix well and boil for 1-2 minutes.

Add milk and mix well. Add sugar, stir and cook till the sugar dissolves. Take the pan off the heat.

Strain the tea in individual serving cups and serve hot.

Crosscountry

Ginger and Cardamom Tea: Adrak ya elaichi? This is the most common question asked before preparing a cup of chai at Indian households. After masala chai, it is safe to say that cardamom or ginger tea are the most popular flavours of chai, enjoyed all over India. During cold winter days, a cup of ginger tea is used as a home remedy to cure a sore throat in a jiffy. Since cardamoms are grown and available in abundance in the Southern part of India, people love their share of this flavourful tea in the South too.

North

Kahwa: Like many other admirable things about 'heaven on Earth' Kashmir, this tea is something Kashmiris love to sip on, almost throughout the year, but more during the super chilly winter months.

The traditional way to prepare it is in a special brass kettle known as samovar with the special Kashmiri green tea leaves, exotic spices, nuts and the 'red gold,' kesar or saffron threads. So, whether you get a chance to visit this picturesque place or not, this beverage is a must-try for all. Here's the recipe for you to try it at home:

INGREDIENTS

2 tsps kahwa tea leaves | 8-10 green cardamoms | 1 cinnamon | A pinch of saffron + for garnishing | 8-10 almonds, chopped | 2 tbsps honey

METHOD

Crush the green cardamoms in a mortar with a pestle.

Add 3 cups water to a deep saucepan. Add crushed cardamoms, cinnamon and saffron and allow the water to come to a boil.

Add tea leaves, almonds and continue to boil for another minute. Add honey and mix well.

Strain into a kettle and pour into individual cups. Garnish with saffron and serve hot.

Noon Chai

A beautiful pink-coloured, salted tea, another traditional jewel from Kashmir, the land of extraordinary beauty. This one's also called shir or gulabi chai because of its pretty pink hue, that it gets from a pinch of baking soda used while brewing it. Its preparation is unique when compared to others and this tea can soothe your senses with its aroma and velvety flavour. I got a chance to visit Kashmir a few years ago on Kargil Diwas to share a conversation and good food with the braveheart soldiers of our country. Like always, I had this urge to explore the local cuisine. So, I went out on a food trail with my team. Along with the other popular dishes, I had always heard and read a lot about the noon chai, but this time, I had an opportunity to actually get a taste of it and experience it in its surroundings, and I wouldn't have missed it for the world. The memories, aroma and flavour of the exceptional noon chai are etched in my memory. And somehow, I managed to take a note of their secret recipe too. Making it is quite simple and I am sharing the traditional recipe right here.

INGREDIENTS

2 tsps tea leaves | A pinch of salt | 1 inch cinnamon | 2 green cardamoms | 1 star anise (phool chakri) | ½ tsp baking soda | 1 cup milk | 2½ tbsps sugar | Powdered pistachios for garnishing | Dried rose petals for garnishing

METHOD

Heat 1½ cups of water in a deep saucepan, add tea leaves and mix well. Bring to a boil.

Add cinnamon, green cardamoms, star anise and mix well. Cook for 1 minute.

Add salt, baking soda and mix well. Add milk and mix well.

Add sugar and cook till the sugar melts. Take the pan off heat.

Strain tea in individual cups, garnish with powdered pistachios and dried rose petals. Serve hot.

Butter tea: A popular tea variety that comes from the Himalayan region, is also known as po cha in Tibet or gur gur chai in Ladakh. This tea is prepared with black tea leaves as the base, along with the addition of yak butter, salt, some milk and water. Making it is a little complex, but the flavour is very special too. It acts as an energy booster and is healthier than many other types of tea. If you ever happen to visit this part of the country, you should definitely take a sip of this chai while enjoying the beautiful mountain views.

East

Ronga Saah: Assam, being the largest producer of tea in India with its beautiful tea gardens, has a special flavour to offer. Also known as lal cha, ronga saah is a red-coloured tea common in Assamese households. It is prepared sans spices and milk and is the simplest one to make. You just need the right tea leaves for it to enjoy the eye-treating red shade. Sugar or no sugar is your choice but enjoying a cup of this special lal rang ki chai is soothing and extremely healthy too. Pretty much the perfect tea for your soul!

West

Irani Chai: There is a very interesting story behind the famed Irani Chai. It is said that the Persians came to Mumbai in search of a better life, then migrated to Pune and landed in Hyderabad, bringing the delish Irani chai with them. Unlike the traditional way of preparing tea, to make this variant, you have to boil the tea leaves and the milk in separate containers. And if you're a true Mumbaikar, you will know that a cup of Irani chai is incomplete without the quintessential bun maska. For several hundred years, the Irani cafes in Mumbai have been serving this exceptional beverage with the same flavour. Time to take a sip of this popular chai in your home kitchen.

INGREDIENTS

½ tbsp tea leaves | 1½ cups milk | 4 tsps sugar

METHOD

Heat milk in a deep saucepan and let it come to boil. Reduce the heat, add sugar and mix. Cook the mixture till it thickens.

Heat 1½ cups water in another saucepan, add the tea leaves and let the mixture boil for 1 minute. Take the pan off heat.

For serving, strain the tea mixture into individual glasses and top with the reduced milk.

Serve hot with bun maska.

Cutting Chai: I feel there's a reason why Mumbai is called 'the city that never sleeps' and that reason is a glass of Cutting Chai. This half-filled glass of tea is enough to wipe off a day full of tensions or stress in a jiffy, while refreshing the senses. Well, the magic not just lies in its preparation but in its quantity. It is said that the chai is enjoyed best when had the 'cutting' way, so that it can be enjoyed more than 2-3 times in a day, in moderation and a guilt-free way! Cutting chai is not just tea, it's a sentiment for all of us and just a sip of it is enough to make you fall in love with it.

South

Sulaimani Chai: This sweet and sour chai is from South India, prepared from black tea without milk. A dash of lemon juice, some sugar and sometimes some whole spices brewed together to a golden gorgeousness is what makes for a perfect cup of Sulaimani Chai. It is said to be made popular by the Arabs who used to visit the Malabar Coast for trade purposes. The Arabian word 'Sulaiman' translates to 'man of peace.' As interesting as its story of origin is, the taste is much better, super hearty and energising. Traditionally, it is served as a digestive beverage after heavy meals like that of a biryani and salan but is also considered an inherent part of Islamic marriages in Kerala.

This is what the story of chai in India looks like! Diverse, rich and distinctive – it is safe to say that India is a country which loves tea a little more than many others. You can visit any part of this country and in every corner, every street and every household, you will definitely find a tea lover who is ready to have a conversation with you, over a pyali of chai! Besides these, here are two of my personal favourites to which, come rain or shine, I'm literally hooked. I'm absolutely in love with these, hope it becomes the same for you.

Gujarati Lemongrass Tea

A lemongrass and ginger flavoured tea, this one's popular at my home. Alyona and I share a cup of this soothing chai every morning. This is her special recipe to help me kick-start my day and I'm sure it will help you too. So, here it goes…

INGREDIENTS

2 tsp tea leaves | 3x2 inch pieces of lemongrass | ½ inch ginger | Milk, optional | Sugar, optional

METHOD

Heat 1 cup water in a deep saucepan. Add lemongrass and ginger, cover and boil for 2-3 minutes.

Add tea leaves, stir and let it boil for 1-2 minutes.

Strain the tea mixture into individual cups. Add milk and sugar as required.

Serve hot.

Masala Lemon Chai

This is another tea enjoyed at my home very often. This one is an instant refresher, detoxifies the body and can comfort a sore throat as well. You can start your morning with a cup of this chai and be energised for the day ahead. I am sharing the recipe below.

INGREDIENTS

1 tsp tea leaves | ½ tsp black pepper powder | ½ tsp cumin (jeera) powder | Black salt to taste | Dash of lemon juice | Sugar, optional

METHOD

Heat 1 cup water in a deep saucepan and bring to a boil.
Add tea leaves, stir and let it boil for 1-2 minutes
Add black pepper powder, cumin powder and black salt. Mix well.
Add lemon juice and let it boil for a minute. Add sugar as required
Strain the tea mixture into individual cups and serve hot.

Tapasya Mundhra, *a Nutritionist by profession is acclaimed as the best Dietician in Delhi. Her achievements in the Healthcare Sector has made her the front runner for many prestigious magazines and News outlets. She aspires to change lives through her many comprehensive Health Programmes. Her achievements in the field of healthcare have made her a favourite choice of many celebrated media houses including the Hindustan Times, NDTV, India Today and Business World etc. She is also a lecturer associated with ACE and she believes in imparting knowledge and experience to future generations She also specialiszes in Cancer Nutrition.*

The Cup of Good
HEALTH

The nutritional value of tea has always been acknowledged and there is a reason why it is very often called a 'cup of good health'. For more than a thousand years, drinking a refreshing cup of tea has been considered a healthy habit and today, evidence supporting this practice can be found. While there are various varieties of tea types available, purists consider only green tea, black tea, white tea, oolong tea, and pu-erh tea the real thing. Distinctive processing of the leaves of the Camellia sinensis plants brings about one-of-a-kind flavour profile of every one of these teas. However, herbal teas like Chamomile and peppermint are the product of roots, leaves, flowers and other components from a variety of plants. Some of major countries that continually influence tea production are China (43 per cent), India (22 per cent), Kenya (8 per cent), Sri Lanka (5 per cent) and Turkey (5 per cent).

In addition to its contribution in overall fluid intake, tea is rich in natural antioxidants due to presence of flavonoids, making it an important dietary source. Tea is a beverage which –when taken on its own – has no calories and when consumed with milk, contributes to daily intake of nutrients.

Polyphenols or flavonoids are what make tea a healthful drink. High content of this bioactive substance makes the beverage rich in antioxidants, antiviral, and causes its anti-inflammatory activities; modulates detoxification enzymes; stimulates immune function and decreases platelet aggregation. Tea also has caffeine and theanine which influences the brain and appear to elevate mental alertness. Black tea has the most noteworthy measure of caffeine proportion when compared with coffee. An 8-ounce cup of black tea has 48 mg caffeine; green tea has 29 mg, Oolong about 38 mg per cup. However, herbal teas may be caffeine free.

Observational research has found that daily consumption of tea is associated with reduced risk of premature death, heart disease, stroke and type two diabetes. Made from steamed tea leaves, green tea has high concentration of Epigallocatechin Gallate (EGCG) and its antioxidants can prevent clogging of the arteries, burn fat, counteract oxidative stress on the brain, reduce risk of neurological disorders like Alzheimer's and Parkinson's diseases, reduce risk of stroke, improve cholesterol levels and may also negatively impact the growth of bladder, *breast*, lung, stomach, pancreatic, and colorectal cancers.

Studies also show that black tea, when consumed with Basil, green cardamoms, neem and other flavours can reduce the risk of stroke and protect lungs from damage caused by exposure to cigarette smoke. The uncured and unfermented white tea has the most potent anticancer properties. A fermented tea, popularly known as Kombucha tea, originated in China or Japan and has been consumed for thousands of years due to being a potential source of probiotics. Tea contains several species of lactic-acid bacteria which can improve many aspects of health, including digestion, inflammation and even weight loss.

Additionally, a simple preparation of pouring hot water over dried herbs, spices, flowers, fruit, seeds, roots, or leaves of various plants popularly known as herbal teas offer extraordinary medical advantages. Chamomile tea or Camomile, known for its calming effects, is useful as a sleep aid; peppermint tea is used to support digestive tract health and has antioxidant, anticancer, antibacterial and antiviral properties. Likewise, ginger and echinacea tea are extremely popular remedies said to prevent and shorten the common cold. A special kind of tea made from the leaves of the rooibos plant benefits bone health. One can easily taste delicious flavours naturally free of sugar and calories in a variety of herbal teas available today worldwide.

Yellow Tea is another unique variety of tea, a drink that is slowly becoming popular across the globe. The health benefits of this tea is somewhat similar to those of

green tea. One of the basic reasons of processing this tea is to remove the grassy aroma of the green tea. This rare expensive tea follows a process similar to that green tea in addition to the 'Sealed Yellowing', were the tea is allowed to oxidise at leisurely pace for a short time to give it the yellowish hue. The leaves then undergo further treatment to preserve the colour and aroma of the dried leaves. Yellow tea, if taken in moderation (should not cross 200mg per day) is good during pregnancy till 12th week. Black, green, and oolong, white tea are all considered safe to consume during pregnancy as long the intake is limited to two cups at the most daily.

While the best time to have black tea is either mornings to kickstart the day or in evening to revitalise the system, green tea with its abundant health benefits can be enjoyed throughout the day.

Oolong tea can be reserved for the mid-morning or late afternoon – a pick-me-up cup due its mild caffeine content! White tea, which undergoes the least processing, has negligible caffeine content and is sun dried to lock in the subtle flavours, is best had with meals or even while relaxing after a long day.

While different benefits are attributed to different teas, it is significant that the beverage must be consumed at the right temperature. Drinking tea that is too hot (130-140° F) can increase the risk of oesophageal and stomach cancers. Another risk is caffeine overload, which may lead to nervousness, restlessness and disturbed sleeping patterns.

Consumption of tea may not be a magic pill, but whether you drink it hot or cold; the benefits of tea go far beyond refreshment.

Rinku Madan is a free spirited Chef / Food Writer living in New Delhi. After her studies in Global Journalism in Harvard, and food writing in New York, she joined CNN International News and went on to becoming Editor, Food-Nightlife for the The Times Of India. Madan writes globally about food and travel.

Tea **PAIRING**

Tea taught me the need to take care of my health, improve my digestion, my skin while giving me a boost of antioxidants to keep my body young and protect it from the damage of pollution. But most importantly, tea inspired me to start living a more grounded life, appreciating the quiet and simple moments and to share great tea with the people I love.

Cup after cup, tea inspired me to look for the story behind all things and food that I buy, learning to consciously select based on the origin, on how sustainable the package is, the quality of the material and ingredients used.

Tea taught me to appreciate simple things while being conscious of the environment and people around me.

When it comes to pairing tea blends with food, learning how to deliciously pair your favourite meals with tea is like learning how to pair a fine wine with a meal or finding the 'right' perfume for yourself.

There are many varieties of tea and it is amazing to know that most of these types come from the same plant. The only difference in these types of teas are where they are grown, how they are harvested, and how they are prepared for brewing. All these tiny details determine the flavour and aroma that make up every different blend of tea. Going out for a great meal, usually the menu is accompanied with a wine suggestion – and that definitely makes a difference! Choosing the right wine enhances the flavours and the elevates the meal to another level.

Technically, there are some basic norms for that, like Red wines should accompany rich, red meat dishes. White wines with white meats, fish and vegetarian dishes. Dessert wines with cheese and dessert etc.

Sometimes people even decide their meal based on their wine preference for the evening, using the meal to accentuate the wine! Similarly, the selection of tea is equally important like wine. Although, tea and food pairing is a relatively new concept, it is surely catching on fast. Many of us are still just beginning to learn the concept of pairing tea with our food. Tea pairing is an art and is evolving rapidly as people are becoming more inclined towards tea for its calming and health reasons. The right tea can truly enhance the taste of the food on the plate and also contribute significantly to our health.

Tea has a diverse and interesting flavour profile – one that is as complex, if not more so, than wine. And in the same way that you can pair wine with food, you can also pair tea with food. You might know this instinctively already, when you crave black tea and toast on the weekend or enjoy the Jasmine green tea served at your local Asian restaurant. The aim of pairing tea with food is to achieve balance and find a match that both enhances the flavour of the dish and the tea. If you're looking for a new way to impress your guests at your next dinner party, or just have a little fun at home, though there should be no rules, as taste is very relative, yet here's a simple guide to pairing tea with food:

Matching the weight and intensity of the dish and the tea

The six types of tea – white, green, yellow, oolong, black, dark – generally become more intense as you go down the spectrum with white tea having the most delicate and subtle flavours and mouthfeel, black and dark teas having the deepest flavours. When pairing a dish with a tea, consider the weight of the dish and what type of tea has a similar intensity. For example, you could match a green tea with white fish, or a black tea with red meat but you wouldn't pair a white tea with a curry as the tea's delicate notes would be overpowered by the strong spice flavours and tastes of the curry.

Finding flavour notes that match the food

You can enhance flavours by choosing a tea that has the same notes as the dish you are drinking it with. For example, A green tea from Japan which has marine and vegetal notes works well with a simple white fish and green vegetable dish.

Find flavour notes that complement the food

If you know food and flavour well, you will understand which different flavours complement each other. Think about different foods that go well together. For example, blue cheese and pear, prosciutto and melon, walnuts and honey, lamb and rosemary, chocolate and cream. Think about flavours that go well with the key ingredients of the dish, then find a tea with those flavours. For example, you could pair a black tea with a caramel and nut tart.

Mouthfeel and texture

The way food feels in your mouth has a dramatic effect on your experience of that food: think crunchy roast vegetables or silky chocolate mousse, slow-cooked lamb. Tea also has texture and the way it feels in your mouth can be – a drying sensation, soft and mellow or full-bodied that coats your mouth etc. A dish that is rich and oily, such as red meat, works really well with a Sri Lankan or Assam black, the high tannin content and astringency could act as a palate-cleanser.

SOME SIMPLE PAIRINGS

WHITE TEA: cucumber salad, mild cheese (e.g. Camembert), pannacotta

GREEN TEA: sushi, fish and steamed greens, plant-based salads, chicken, rice

LIGHT OOLONG: scallops, lobster, prawns, fruit salad

DARK OOLONG: duck, smoked/cured meat, roasted vegetables, granola/muesli, pancakes with maple syrup

BLACK TEA: red meat, chocolate, pastries, rich deserts

DARK/FERMENTED: red meat, cheese (or after food as a digestif)

Experimentation is the best way to find out what would work best for you. The suggestions above could help as a guide but sometimes, you will find an unexpected combination works beautifully.

When in doubt though, black tea goes with everything!

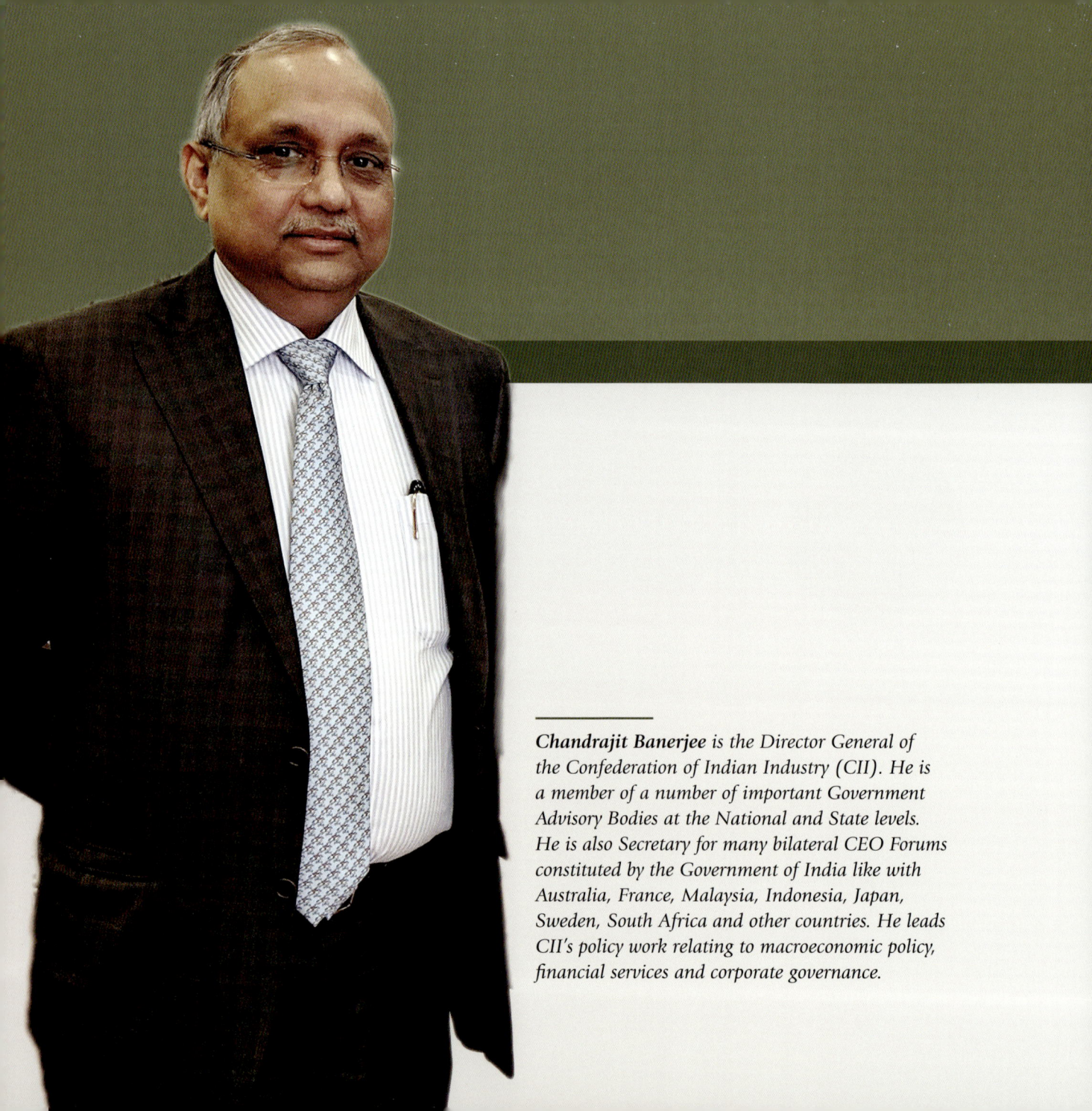

Chandrajit Banerjee is the Director General of the Confederation of Indian Industry (CII). He is a member of a number of important Government Advisory Bodies at the National and State levels. He is also Secretary for many bilateral CEO Forums constituted by the Government of India like with Australia, France, Malaysia, Indonesia, Japan, Sweden, South Africa and other countries. He leads CII's policy work relating to macroeconomic policy, financial services and corporate governance.

The Role Of Tea In The Indian **ECONOMY**

As a Bengali with links with Darjeeling, it's a no-brainer that one is a genuine tea-addict. The day starts and ends with tea – also many cups in between!

Any visit to an office or a home in India invariably takes place over a cup of tea. No meeting is complete without tea being served and factories will always slot in time for workers to have a tea break. Inextricably linked with the Indian culture of hospitality, availability of tea is never a problem anywhere in the country, be it a roadside tea stall or a high-class tea boutique.

But, without delving much into the romanticism of tea, let me come to the subject of this article. India is the second largest producer of this commodity, which is brewed into one of the most widely consumed and most popular beverages in the world.

The country is also one of the largest tea consuming nations globally, with around three-fourths of its total produce making its way into homes across the country. Indian tea is among the world's finest, known for the wide variety of aromas, flavours, colours and strengths.

The Indian tea industry is nearly 200 years old. Large-scale production of tea in India was started by the British East India Company and as the area under tea bushes increased, India became one of the largest tea producers in the world by the 1850s. Its cool rolling hillsides in different parts of the country, advantageous rainfall patterns and large workforce make it the perfect place to plant different varieties of tea bushes. As the price of tea leaves came down, the contribution of this beverage – that was rapidly gaining popularity in the world – to India's economy grew immensely. Favourable agro-climatic conditions, availability of modern and upgraded manufacturing facilities, heavy investments in tea processing units, and strong research and innovation are some of the key factors that have placed the Indian tea industry at the leading position in the world.

India is home to some of the best and the most popular varieties of tea in the world, ranging from the aromatic Darjeeling tea, the strong Assam tea, and the gentle Nilgiri tea as well as the relatively new variants such as green tea and white tea. Assam, Darjeeling, Sikkim, Nilgiris, and Kangra are some of the top tea-growing regions in the country, producing high quality, specialty teas that have built a strong brand image for the country across the world.

Apart from bringing joy to millions of tea drinkers the world over, the agri-product is a significant contributor to the Indian economy in three key ways. First, it adds to the national agricultural income and overall GDP of the country. Secondly, it earns valuable foreign exchange for India. Third, and most important, the tea plantations are a source of livelihood for millions of workers, their families and other workers dependent on the upstream industry.

The total turnover of the Indian tea industry is estimated at around Rs 10,000 crores. India was the second largest tea producer in the world after China in 2019, recording a production of 1,340 million kilograms. Since 2007-08, production has expanded by almost two-fifths, attesting to the continued rising taste for tea. With better technologies and productivity, yields of our plantations have gone up by 30 per cent in this period.

Indian tea exports have steadily gone up over the years and contributed significantly to the country's gross domestic product (GDP). While black tea is predominant in India's exports, it has also increased its sales of green tea. In 2019, India's tea exports were valued at around US$ 814 million, accounting for more than 11per cent of world's total. India is the world's third largest exporter of tea, after China and Kenya. Iran, Russia, United States, United Kingdom and the United Arab Emirates were the top 5 export destinations during 2019. Catering to a diverse international market, the tea industry is a major source of foreign exchange for the country and is also a substantial revenue earner for the Government.

State/Region wise Tea Production data for the year 2019-20 & 2020-21 -- Qty. in M.Kgs									
	2019-20			2020-21			Difference in 2020-21 over 2019-20		
State / Region	BG	SG	Total	BG	SG	Total	BG	SG	Total
Assam Valley	342.38	309.05	651.43	296.75	288.76	585.51	-45.63	-20.29	-65.92
Cachar	43.37	0.58	43.95	39.34	1.38	40.72	-4.03	0.80	-3.23
Total Assam	**385.75**	**309.63**	**695.38**	**336.09**	**290.14**	**626.23**	**-49.66**	**-19.49**	**-69.15**
Dooars	130.66	104.97	235.63	122.24	106.18	228.42	-8.42	1.21	-7.21
Terai	43.77	128.64	172.41	40.43	120.46	160.89	-3.34	-8.18	-11.52
Darjeeling	7.75	0.10	7.85	6.55	0.19	6.74	-1.20	0.09	-1.11
Total West Bengal	**182.18**	**233.71**	**415.89**	**169.22**	**226.83**	**396.05**	**-12.96**	**-6.88**	**-19.84**
Others	10.11	19.31	29.42	9.57	18.95	28.52	-0.54	-0.36	-0.90
Total North India	**578.04**	**562.65**	**1140.69**	**514.88**	**535.92**	**1050.80**	**-63.16**	**-26.73**	**-89.89**
Tamil Nadu	60.45	95.55	156.00	63.98	96.06	160.04	3.53	0.51	4.04
Kerala	47.65	11.61	59.26	53.87	12.98	66.85	6.22	1.37	7.59
Karnataka	4.61	0.25	4.86	5.08	0.26	5.34	0.47	0.01	0.48
Total South India	**112.71**	**107.41**	**220.12**	**122.93**	**109.30**	**232.23**	**10.22**	**1.89**	**12.11**
Total All India	**690.75**	**670.06**	**1360.81**	**637.81**	**645.22**	**1283.03**	**-52.94**	**-24.84**	**-77.78**

Source: Tea Board of India

BG - Big Growers; SG - Small Growers

LIFE IN A CUPPA

The Indian tea industry is highly labour intensive and is a large-scale provider of employment in the country, offering livelihood opportunities directly to more than one million people, with half of the workforce constituting women. With areas of work that range from plantation work, processing, auctioning, branding, marketing and research, the industry offers a wide variety of opportunities for gainful employment in associated sectors.

The lush tea gardens and tea estates of India are some of the most beautiful and must-see places and attract tourists from all over the country as well as the world. The tea gardens offer personal visits, tea tasting and trekking on tea trails, and many other recreational activities. Some of the most popular and most visited tea estates in the country can be found in Darjeeling, Munnar, Assam, Nilgiri, and Wayanad, among others.

With world tea consumption expected to grow further in the coming years, fuelled by demand from major markets like China and other emerging countries, the Indian tea industry has further potential to grow with many opportunities on offer.

As more and more innovative variants enter the market, such as green and white tea, the tea industry has further scope of expanding and diversifying as well. The new variants are also gaining popularity in the market owing to their immunity boosting properties and the rising health and wellness awareness amongst today's youth. India's masala chai, for example, infused with ancient herbs and spices, has reinvented itself as a sought-after health drink for millennials.

Stronger market promotion and branding can further boost the growth of the industry. The Tea Board of India, set up in 1953, undertakes direct promotional activities including organising international trade fairs and exhibitions, arranging buyer-seller meets and sending and hosting trade delegations. Research and innovation, market development and surveys to analyse consumer behaviour and diversify product offerings can further rebrand Indian teas for global markets.

The growing tea industry of India is one of our natural advantages and can continue to capture the imagination of consumers in all parts of the world, while contributing to India's economy and employment.

So, cheers over a cup of tea!

Sangeeta Kichlu *has the distinction of being the first accredited Lady Tea Taster in India. It is not surprising that Sangeeta spends her life immersed in tea. She was born in Margherita, Assam where her father was the Manager of a group of tea estates and went to school in Shillong. Carries on the family tradition, she joined the tea profession in 1979 and has since worked for many leading tea companies. Working in the UK, early in her career, for leading Tea Brokers Thompson Lloyd & Ewart and having a brief stints at Tetley Tea and with German buyers in Hamburg, Sangeeta had exposure to international origin tea and buyers at the start of her working life. She has chaired several committees including the CTTA (Calcutta Tea Traders Association), being the first lady professional to chair this steering committee comprising Producers, Auctioneers and Buyers.*

The Importance Of Being A Tea **TASTER**

The phrase 'Tea Taster' or 'Tea Sommelier' as we call ourselves today, conjures up an image of mystical, exotic skills. And I would like to assure you, that it is exactly so! The Tasters sip, slurp and spit are the hallmark of assurance of quality! Tasters are often termed as the 'holy cows' of the tea business.

'I say, let the world go to hell, but I should always have my tea'—Anonymous …and thus I embraced the profession of a Tea Taster, having been born on a tea estate and finally, completing the circle by marrying a Tea Taster too!

Tea Tasting is an intense refinement or sensitising of one's olfactory and visual skills – those of the tongue, nose and eyes and then using the sum of these senses in the backdrop of the consumption of tea – to reach a conclusion on the quality of a particular cup of tea.

This comes from years of experience and aptitude, married with knowledge on tea growing, manufacture, blending and consumer tastes.

Tea as a drink is both historical and futuristic. It has evolved from a rare drink, available to only a few to a 'Universal Drink' cutting across ethnic and socio-economic barriers. In all this the Tea Taster's role has been critical.

Tea was accidentally discovered and, in the beginning,, it was purely a medicinal drink consumed for its curative elements.

The taste of this camellia sinensis leaf brewed with hot water was good and thus found its way into the Emperor's courts as a rare, privileged brew.

Tea has travelled a long way since. Whilst the exotic brew continues to be manufactured and drunk, a drink for the common man.

The Tea Taster is the backbone of the entire Tea Supply Chain…from the grower to the consumer. The evolution of tea from medicinal, to exotic to convivial to cool has been done with tea tasters guiding producers on the type of teas to grow and make.

A Tea Taster
Sees the leaf.
Sees and smells the infusion.
Sees, smells and tastes the cup.
This is the process of professional tea tasting.

When tea is grown and processed in the tea factory, the Tea Taster located at the production point tastes the tea for full quality control. Through years of tasting and growing and factory processing knowledge, by slurping and tasting the tea, the taster is able to identify the area of correctness and faults. A good tea will be flavoury, with a good nose, good colour whilst a faulty one may be described as under withered or over-fermented or over fired or simply tea made from bad leaf. Thus, the taster's role at origin is to ensure that each tea estate

and factory makes a product that realises its full potential through good plucking and good tea manufacturing. All this, in turn, is guided by market forces as the type of tea that is made is dependent on which market this produce is targeted for. This information comes from the Tea Brokers & Auctioneers and Tea Marketers.

A Taster working in a Tea Broking and Auctioning Company may be described as the valuer of tea produce. A Tea Taster is the median between the grower and the buyer and tastes teas of multiple tea companies and multiple origins and is thus able to give a comparative quality and price evaluation. This is done when samples reach broking houses for sale in the Tea Auctions. On a single day, a taster may taste up to 2,000 cups of tea and put a price on each tea. Cleaning of the pallet with water is required to remove the pallet fatigue that comes with tasting hundreds of cups. The tea is valued, based on the inherent quality and the suitability of the tea for a specific market. When a tea is made for a market that pays a higher price, the tea is more valuable. For example, the Long-Leaved Orthodox teas which may be totally desired and in high demand in the

high-consumption Middle East markets have no value in the Indian subcontinent.

A Tea Broker & Auctioneer has on his platform hundreds of tea estates and 300 to 400 buyers buying tea. With years of tasting, it is the skill of identifying the relevant buyers for every single tea that is being put up for sale. Quality and buying pattern is very dynamic, changing from year to year and from season to season. Building this into the tea valuation separates a good taster/valuer from an ordinary one. This tasting happens throughout the year, as there are 52 Tea Sales and Auctions in a year.

The Taster who is a Tea Buyer, after tasting most of the teas that the Auctioneer has offered, will make herself/ himself present in the weekly auctions to buy teas required for his/her specific target markets (different destination in India and across the world), as well as for their packets, if they are in the branded retail business. It is these tea buyers who buy the best/ most suitable teas at the cheapest price possible. This ability comes from years of tea tasting and understanding what the competition is likely to select, pay and buy.

The Taster as Wholesale Tea Marketer must know which tea is suitable for which country and the markets propensity to pay. For example, there are countries, across the Middle East and Russia, large consumers of tea, who drink this beverage without milk. Here, it is the traditional, old fashioned, Orthodox Leaf Teas that are exported to these destinations. Similarly, the British & Irish, the Indians and Pakistanis, all large consumers of tea, must have their tea with milk. Thus, the CTC, grainy, cut teas that make a thicker cup of tea must be sold here. The colour, thickness and taste preferences again vary from region to region and across multiple income brackets. All these factors are taken into account whilst tasting, valuing, offering and selling teas in these markets. This comes from years of tasting experience, market knowledge, and intensive travel to target markets.

On the subject of 'milky tea'– this beverage is popular across India today when tea is drunk with milk and tons of sugar. The British established expansive commercial plantations in Assam, Dooars, Darjeeling, the Nilgiris and Munnar in the 1900s. There weren't enough people interested in drinking tea in India even when the country was free in 1947, because at that time, it was traditionally made – loose leaf tea, brewed with hot water. Thus, in 1950s was created the CTC tea process. It is only thereafter that tea was mass popularised in India, UK and Pakistan and is today our National Drink. The popularity of Indian "Chai" has today taken the world by storm.

The Taster as the Tea Blender is the next in the supply chain of tea. The taster's role as a blender is to ensure 'consistency of quality. Tea is very seasonal in quality. Tea quality varies with each growing origin, each estate. Basically, the natural elements cause tea to be extremely inconsistent and thus the tea taster's role here is to reach a consistent result, throughout the year by picking the varying tea constituents to produce a tea for a packet…like say Tata Gold or Red Label that has to taste the same throughout the year.

Within the quality, the price of tea has to be managed too. The Tea Blender is the last tea tasting sentinel in the tea tasting supply chain, only to be checked after this randomly by Tea Quality Controllers who are tea tasters too.

The term Tea Sommelier (borrowed from a wine taster) is very new – it is not a more than 16-17-years-old phrase, I think. In fact, when I decided to call myself a 'Tea Sommelier 'in 2004, I had not seen this phrase anywhere. The reason I used this phrase was because I was working with Luxury Hotels training their Food and Beverage Personnel on the fine attributes of tea, the nuances, and the many elements of taste that determined the quality of tea. Whilst the Wine Sommelier had made deep forays into the hospitality business by this time, there was practically a non-existence of tea tasters working with the hospitality business and tea connoisseurs, who were ever so curious to know more about tea. Today, happily, this curiosity for tea has grown manifold and so have the presence of 'Tea Sommeliers'. The 'Tea Sommelier' is really at the end of the supply chain – albeit the specialty, discerning chain.

Tea is drunk across all income levels, all countries, thus a Tea Tasters profession with Tea Travels, takes you across a myriad of cultures, countries making ' tea friends that last a lifetime. After Sipping, Slurping and Spitting till my teeth are red, I would say – the life of a Tea Taster is blessed.

As long as we drink tea, there is no substitute for the Tea Taster. Chemical analysis can help determine the constituents of tea but to judge tea in its totality, imbibing habits, health and culture will remain a taster's monopoly. A computer may help mankind to do his thinking but it is unlikely that the Tea Tasters palate can be replaced to ensure that you get the right cup of tea! A Tea Taster is the guiding light in the evolution of tea.

'Each Cup of Tea represents an imaginary voyage'—Catherine Douzel.

If you are cold; Tea will warm you: If you are heated; Tea will cool you: If you are depressed, it will cheer you. If you are excited; Tea will calm you.

Examples of a Tea Sommeliers Description of Tea	
Tea Tasters Expression	**Tea Sommeliers Expression**
Light. Flavoury.	A Delicate, champagne coloured brew with floral notes. Suitable at tea time with Madeline Cakes or Dinner with Light White Fish
Strong. Brisk	A full, wholesome strong brew. Suitable early in the morning as a Wake Up tea. Suitable for pairing with red meats.
Malty, Bright	A creamy orange liqour, infused with a red earthy flavour typical of a Good Assam 2nd flush. Leaves the mouth creamy and satisfied.
Light, White Tea	A delicate silvery liqour with thin grassy notes. Gentle on the palate. Suitable for pairing with Sushi.

Larry Brown is a Planter, Tea Maker, Engineer, Taster and Blender and Inventor, Having travelled to India in 1960 from Ireland, he has travelled to many lands and has been tea planter in Assam, West Bengal, Papua New Guinea and a Plantation owner in Australia. His experiences in the tea ecosystem and his narrative is a visual treat as we accompany him on his journey from his native land to the highlands in India.

The Ghost Of Namdang Factory **BUNGALOW**

I have been 'in Tea' a long time, in fact, I don't think I will ever leave and even at this ripe old age, believe you me I have a tea project planned!

It all started when I joined the Sirocco Engineering Works in Belfast as an Office Boy at the tender age of 15 years.

Sirocco was one of the only two major manufacturers of Tea machinery, the other being Marshall's, Britannia Engineering Works in Gainsborough in England.

Samuel Cleland Davidson was the Founder of Sirocco in 1881. He went to Cachar in Bengal when he was only 17, to assist his cousin James who owned a number of Gardens in Assam and Cachar. Samuel later owned his own gardens.

While an Apprentice with Sirocco, I was awarded a Tea Traineeship and was thus being trained to become either as a Sales Engineer in one of the Overseas Depots or as a Tea Factory Engineer. This traineeship covered all aspects of tea machinery fabrication and construction, tea machinery design in the Drawing Office, Fan testing, Electrical – the lot!

In 1960, a request from two overseas Tea Companies came – one from Nyasaland (present day Malawi) and the other from the Namdang Tea Company who had gardens in Assam. Thank goodness I chose the latter.

When I had made my choice, the Sirocco Directors called me to a meeting where some waxed poetic about their days in India and how I was following the footsteps of the Founder, Sam Davidson, and we all sipped glasses of Champagne.

There followed a meeting and interview with the Namdang Board in London's Mincing Lane and a Medical Examination – and I was given the all clear.

Leaving Belfast's Queen's Quay on the Duke of Lancaster, bound for Heysham, I cast wistful looks at the receding Queens Bridge and thought it might be some years before I see this again and although I had read up some on Assam, I wondered how I would fare.

From Heysham, I travelled to Stoke and Trent to visit family and after a week or so there, it was off to board another ship – a bit bigger this time – the Anchor Line's Caledonia, a 10,000 tonner that would take me to India.

The Caledonia would take 19 days to get to Bombay and the route was by Gibralatar, Port Said, Karachi and finally to Bombay.

After leaving Liverpool, it was around dinner time that we were crossing the Bay of Biscay – it had a reputation that was evident when only six passengers turned up for dinner. I was one of them as I had been in many small boats in rough seas and had good sea legs. When I walked to and from my cabin, I could hear many poor people retching and rueing the sea trip.

Shipboard life was interesting and I met many interesting people and some returning Tea Planters. I was most impressed when in a group, a planter spoke to an orderly, saying,, 'Bearer, ek, do tin, char, panch, mitha pani lao'!

I made friends with two young bankers who had been on a training course with National & Grindlays and were returning to the Branches in their respective countries. Ravi Madhok was returning to Delhi and Nazir Chinoy to Karachi. I kept in touch with both Ravi and Nazir for many years. We also had a young teenager, Idris, who tagged along with us and I later found out he was related to King Idris of Libya, who, while at a bath house in Cairo, was deposed by Muammar Gaddafi.

The stops at Gibraltar and Port Said were fascinating – Barbary Apes and then the Pyramids! Simon Artz and Gully Gully men.

When we arrived in Karachi, Nazir suggested that I stay with his family as the Caledonia would be docked overnight. This short stay was to be my first experience of actually setting foot in the Orient and I loved every minute of it. Nazir's parents were lovely and when his niece called in to say hello, I thought she was the most beautiful girl I had ever seen and fell instantly in love.

I had to ask Nazir if the many little geckos I saw for the first time in my bedroom were dangerous. When he took me around places to see in Karachi, I had never seen so many people or experienced such sights, sounds, smells and colours in all my life – it was fantastic.

The next evening, as the Caledonia was appraching Bombay, nature put on a show and hundreds of shooting stars crossed the sky. I was seeing many wonderful things and I'm sure there was more to come.

The Company had arranged for me to be taken care of regarding accommodation, luggage and the onward train journey to Calcutta.

I stayed in the Taj and marvelled at the view, how everything in the hotel was ornate, opulent and ivory coloured but I wanted to get out to walk the streets and see everything and I did just that.

The next morning, a Mr Chidambaram took me to the central station and made sure I was safely seated on the train that would take me to Calcutta – a three-day journey.

Every bit of the journey so far had been so exciting and when the train set off, I looked forward to seeing much of the different scenery I would witness. I was also adventurous with the array of food that was served on the train – but unfortunately, I drank the chilled water that was proffered.

Prior to leaving the UK, I was given a small page of notes prepared by Mrs Natalie Kilburn, the wife of a Namdang Director. It had a list of useful items to take to India and there was a little cautionary note that went like this:

Luscious Fruits and Salads Green
Harbour deadly germs unseen
The Traveller in the East must not
Eat anything unless it's hot.

Sadly, the caring Mrs Kilburn didn't tell me about the water. What was to have been a leisurely journey across India, drinking in all the sights (no pun intended), had ended with me drinking the water. The less said about the journey the better… but the inconvenience would continue for some time!

When I was met in Calcutta and taken to the Grand Hotel on Chowringhee, I relaxed somewhat but there was an invitation awaiting me in the Hotel to attend a Dinner at Sirocco's Calcutta Office in Middleton Row that was to welcome Miss Sally Maguire who was visiting and she was the daughter of Ted Maguire, the Chairman of Sirocco in Belfast.

I had associated my problem with the Curries and not the water, so I was now very wary of spicy Indian food!

At the Welcoming Dinner Party, curry was served. Very early the next morning, I was taken to Dum Dum Airport and put on board a Douglas DC3 that would take me to Mohanbari Airport near Dibrugarh. It was not a pleasant trip; In April, I had foolishly put on a suit and long trousers as I thought that might be expected attire. In the unpressurised cabin, my ears were paining and wouldn't clear and my stomach queasiness was still with me. My troubles momentarily left me when I saw the magnificent snow-clad Himalayas but

I was about to touch down in Assam an almost physical wreck.

I was met at the Airport by two wonderful people, Simon Penney and Austin Rufus. They immediately made me feel at ease and assured me my problems will be quickly fixed and with that assurance we set off for Margherita. Paddy fields, Banana plants and other different plants, trees and birds, myriads of butterflies, elephants on the road – my problems again disappeared.

On arrival at Namdang I was taken to the Factory Bungalow and everyone fussed over me. The Acting Manager, Chris Gathorne welcomed me, as did Polly Rajpal. Another Assistant, Krishna Kumar who had been to Queens University in Belfast welcomed me, but it was with some trepidation I accepted his invitation to dinner that evening….

I was initially to be Chowkidar at the Manager's Bungalow and live in their house while he and his wife were on six months leave. It was a palace.

While living at the Bara Bungalow in 1960, I saw my first snake crossing the expansive lawn. I ran after it to get a better look, but it turned round started chasing me. I quickly went into the bungalow and got the 12 bore my brother had given me when I left Belfast. I cautiously approached the snake and as it turned and raised up I saw it's hood and knew it was a Cobra. As I went nearer pointing the gun at it and peering down the side to get a better look my finger involuntarily pulled on the trigger as venom splashed on the front gun sight and barrels. It was a spitting Cobra, I later found out but I was sorry that my curiosity had killed the poor snake.

Namdang Factory Bungalow 1960s

Namdang bordered the nearby Patkai Hills and every day the troops of Hoolock Gibbons set up a cacophony of whooping cries. Hornbills and masses of other birds were there. Butterflies in their hundreds. The Hills were teeming with wildlife and although designated as NEFA (North East Frontier Agency) and out of bounds, some of us went over the fence and into the hills and across Rope Bridges and visited Naga villages. We always carried some tea, and this was welcomed by any village or villager we encountered.

River trips on the Tirap, Namchik and Burhi Dehing were magic – monkeys swimming across the river, leopards, elephants, a pack of wild dogs – and the fishing was good. It's sad to think that the young assistants now in tea will miss out on what we were able to witness in the 1960s.

I used the gun my brother gave me only once more:

When I left Belfast, my brother, who was a keen fly fisherman and he liked to collect an assortment of feathers and such so that he could make his own flies. He said that Jungle Fowl in India had a particularly nice plumage and should I ever come across any, their feathers would be welcomed.

As it so happened, while I was living in the Bara Bungalow, I noticed a group of these 'Jungli Murghis (wild fowls)' at a small stream at the bottom of the Bungalow Teela (hillock). One Sunday morning, I went down with the gun, crossed the little bridge and looked at the group of Murghis a short distance away. I thought shooting them on the ground was a bit unsporting, so I clapped my hands – nothing happened. Louder this time-and nothing happened. I finally threw a stone at them and bang, bang, I got Five. I took them down to Chris and Pam's and Chris said, 'Terrific, I'll get Pam to make a good Curry and get some over to enjoy – where did you get them?' I said it's funny you should mention it but it was just at a little stream near the Bara Bungalow. Chris visibly wilted – and then laughed!

'Good God' he said, 'Marion has been hand feeding those birds for years!' Then he added, 'but, we'll enjoy them and keep it a secret' – and the secret was kept. I enjoyed my work and during the Flushes, a lot of leaf came into the factory that sometimes did not stop, and this was usually because the drying capacity in most factories was inadequate. Particularly, during the 'Rains', when 1,000 maunds of green leaf came in, the Factory Assistants called it, Ek Hazar Bimar. The Namdang and Bogapani factories in my day had Coal-Fired Lancashire Boilers that powered Vertical Steam Engines from which their exhaust steam went to radiators for drying. Some old hands told me of a trick to keep up with drying the tea was to hang a weight on the Boiler's Safety Valve – which I did occasionally! I even shovelled coal into the furnace to show the Stokers, how it's done!

I also remember at Bogapani, holding the Electric Distribution Board Main Switches in, with a stout length of bamboo. The Board glowed Red and one could have made toasted bread! Thankfully, tea factories are now all state-of -the-art and such things do not occur.

When as a young apprentice in Sirocco, I was filing the brass-curved battens for fixing to the Tea Roller Brass Table, they had many names but two – Talwar and Boomerang – always stuck in my mind and little did I know that I would see both items and live in both lands. I am fortunate in having been able to visit many lands and learn about the different ways to make tea. I am fortunate too in having been able to stand on a still, warm day, surrounded by tea bushes watching the heat shimmer and savour the delicate fragrances of the Chlorophylls, Linalools and Geraniols –and in the factory, the fresh aroma of the newly macerated leaf, and then the different one during Fermentation when searching for the 'nose' to tell when it should go to the drier, then the clank, clank of the drier trays and the unsurpassable smell of freshly dried tea – and the minor discomfort of tea fibre down the back of one's neck is not a distraction.

It is while sitting on a upturned tea chest in the factory in the morning early hours that I have looked at machinery, and thought of ways to improve performance. One that I came up with in 1963 was the best and I tried to patent it. Remfrys in Calcutta worked on this, but as an assistant I ran out of money and couldn't complete the trials. It was basic simplicity – a plastic roller of varying diameter – install it above the conveyors, shakers, sorters –rub the roller with terylene to charge it and presto, it attracts the tea fibre but not the tea! It is now in use all over the world!

I have not said much about Tea Manufacture and I am familiar with many, like Hand Rolling, Orthodox, CTC (Crush Tear Curl), LTP (Lawrie Tea Processor), Legg Cut plus some different processes for Green tea, Hot Panning, Steam and even experimenting with Microwaves to arrest the polyoxides enzyme but there is still a lot to learn. Mr Ukers (William Harrison, 1935) wrote a book and its title was, All about Tea. I don't think anyone will ever know everything about Tea, but no doubt there will be constant innovations. A tea factory of today is a very different from the ones that I experienced, but the aims were the same – to make the Best tea.

Being in India and on tea plantations were the happiest days in my life and friends made then are lifelong friends and when we visit each other in each other's countries, we talk about those good, happy times- and we have stories; I will close with one that Kakoli liked!

When I moved from the Burra Bungalow at Namdang and was sharing stay with Polly in the Factory Bungalow, he and I would often be asked by the senior planters of the district, 'Have you seen the Ghost?'

Polly and I laughed about this and paid no attention. However, one night, I had just got into bed, ready to go to sleep, when Jimmy Beven drove past en route to the Teela Bungalow where he lived. As was usual for Jim, he sat on the horn as he drove past our bungalow in his big white monster of a Buick or Dodge! At that time, he was courting Jean Filshill, whom he later married. Jean was Matron of the Digboi

On a quick visit to Namdang Bara Bungalow 2014

Hospital and was a lovely, lovely person. Anyway, I ruffled up my pillow, looked at my watch, saw it was 1 am and thought Jim has had a long courting session, plonked my head on the pillow – and froze!

Starting from my ankles I could feel every hair standing on end. I tried to raise myself but couldn't move. Out of the corner of my eye I saw a luminous figure gliding into the room. I shut my eyes and tried to move but I couldn't.

The apparition glided across the floor and while I was praying to Jesus to make him go away – I was absolutely terrified – it leaned on the bedstead end and leaned forward to look at my face. By this time, I was talking and asking him to please go away. He looked at me again and then I felt his presence receding – passing through the closed door. I lay there calling myself a wimp, etc. and on the count of three, I jumped out of bed and switched on the light. There was nothing, but I left the light on all night.

In the morning, when Polly and I were having breakfast, I asked him if he had noticed anything strange about last night – he said yes, 'something threw me out of bed, and it took me some time to get to sleep again'.

As I later learnt, 'he' the ghost, had been a young man who had caught blackwater fever at Namtok and was brought to Namdang. He was put in the same room and the same bed that Polly was sleeping on, and he died.

The story didn't end there because a couple of years later, when I was the sole occupant of the Factory Bungalow he kept visiting me, sometimes three times a week. I think there was a special affinity between us as I had been told that 'he' had died when he was 23 – I too was 23 when I first moved into the Factory Bungalow.

He started visiting in March and thereafter paid me regular visits. On these occasions my dog would get its hackles up and slink away. I would get an icy feeling on my cheek when I was reading a book or listening to music, and enjoying a roaring fire as was normal in the cold weather but he kept on visiting me and I knew he was there when he brought that coldness.

Eventually, I spoke to him and told him

Namdang Factory Bungalow courtesy: Larry Brown

that he was a young planter who had been on the Namtok outgarden, and when he was sick he was brought to the Factory Bungalow and had died from blackwater fever in the bed in the next room.

I walked into the room and showed him the bed and told him if I could help in any way I would do so, but I also told him that he was scaring me out of my skin and that he should leave me alone. I asked if he was satisfied with my explanation. He never returned.

I later learned from the servants of many 'happenings' at the bungalow but I was happy that the tormented soul was at last at rest.

POSTSCRIPT

Jimmy Beven visited Namdang in November 2006. I phoned him from Australia and I naturally enquired about the ghost, and apparently, he's still there! I, obviously, didn't exorcise him completely and he still continues to send shivers down the spines of young assistants!!

I visited Namdang in December 2014, after an absence of 54 years and I went to the Factory Bungalow, which now had a new kitchen and airconditioning –a complete renovation. I visited the bedroom where the young man had died- -it was very still and quiet and I felt that he was still there. Apologies for rambling on perhaps too much –I get carried way when I think of those great times, the friends, the situations, and TEA.

Suhel Seth *is founder of the consultancy firm Counselage India, a branding and marketing consultancy. He advises Chairmen and CEOs of companies across the globe. He is a well-known television commentator and has over 4.7 million followers on Twitter. He is an author of three national best-seller books; and is a prolific actor both on stage and screen.*

Of Tea **TALES**

I had to fall in love with tea. I had no choice. When you are born and raised in Calcutta, tea becomes an integral part of your being: it defines moments; it adds to celebrations and it measures your success. Calcutta was the temple of tea. Clubs like the CC&FC were infested with those from the tea trade. We looked upon them as the epitome of success. Traders and tasters alike. They lived in the best homes; they entertained in the most gracious manner and were almost like a benevolent Mafia if there can ever be one.

The ones who belonged to the business of tea were as interesting as those who made tea their leitmotif: the quintessential 'adda' in Calcutta was born and nurtured by tea. Long before a certain Gujarati made it popular by coining 'Chai pe Charcha': we knew the art of 'charcha' before it became a parody of a political tool. The 'adda' was the heartbeat of Calcutta and contrary to popular perception, the 'adda' was not confined to street sides and their ilk.

It was found in the venerable Bengal Club with as much flair as in Sutripti, a café that was the size of a large shoebox. But what mattered was the tea you had: not the discussions around Malraux and Marx.

Then there were the times of day when tea would be your calling in Calcutta. If you went for a morning walk around Victoria Memorial, you would eventually wind up, post your walk, at the many tea stalls that dotted the area. And people would walk as far as to Bhowanipore to Sharma's for their morning cuppa: but then it wouldn't be tea alone: you would also end up sampling their other wares such as the ubiquitous singhara (known as Samosa in less refined parts of India) as also the poori-bhaji. But tea was what attracted you as it led to heated conversations ranging from the weather or planning to pull down the Government to critiquing a new Satyajit Ray film.

And when you ever had the misfortune of entering a Government office you had to be mindful of the sacredness of the tea ceremony which essentially was an excuse for those mandarins to walk away from their desks and do no work until they had savored their cups of tea. Tea was the perfect ruse to do things that would please your soul regardless of the inconvenience it caused to the others. But then such was the romance of tea.

You also had society tea parties, which would put a Fortnum & Mason to shame: these were society events where you'd be served everything with the finesse of a Bond movie. From finger sized sandwiches to scones and clotted cream to tea served in the finest china. These were by-invitation events which meant that in order to be invited you had to belong. It is at these parties where the first flush of the finest Darjeeling would be unveiled and you partook of it, as it was another kind of baptism. Such was the sanctity of tea in those times.

We never imagined a world, which would embrace green tea or tulsi tea and such like. Today people add more milk to their tea than there is of human kindness. And sugar nowadays leaves a bitter taste if you were to ever offer it to someone.

Gone are the days when you walk into tea shops and ask for your personal blend. Brands of packaged tea stormed that last bastion of personalisation. So now you don't even know the kind of tea you are drinking. We made tea become so impersonal. And then came Starbucks and dislodged tea from its pinnacle of human endeavor.

The world, and sadly India, has moved on from there to the deep morasses of incivility as far the drinking of tea is concerned. We converted a jewel into a plastic toy. We commoditized tea like never before. Today the tea gardens are a pale shadow of themselves. The broking houses no longer have their executive dining rooms and their chummeries. Health aficionados have heaped further desecration on tea by talking about the health benefits of tea and making it sound almost medicinal.

But all is not lost. Whenever I return to Calcutta these days, tea and tea stalls remain my haunts. The ghosts of fine conversation and contrarian views continue to emerge and we take them with a pinch of sugar. We delight ourselves in reliving those moments when a harmless tea cup would kick up a storm of opinion. When tea would be more valuable than some odd tipple. We still look for the same folks who rustled up tea as if it were born in a Michelin-starred kitchen. It is these memories that keep my love for tea unchanged.

Let's Turn The Clock **BACK**

Kakoli G

The finest tea gardens across the globe from the Far East to West Africa all have one feature in common. Tea is cultivated in a wet and temperate climate – long sunny days, rainy nights and pristine mountain breeze. The processing, maturity and form of the leaf gives tea its taste and the region in which it is grown gives its character. The most exotic tea comes from just five countries – Sri Lanka, China, Taiwan, India and Japan.

Chinese Empror Shen Nung (2732 BC)

Bodhidharma (520 AD)

Chinese emperor Huizong (Hui-tsung)

CHINA

Documentary evidence suggests, tea was discovered in China, the first tea drinking nation in the world, way back in 350 BC.

Whatever the origins of tea, it is widely accepted that the Chinese, and tribes from the Indo-China hill regions of Burma, Siam and Cambodia had all discovered the secret of infusing tea leaves with boiling water at least 2,000 years ago. Pinyin Shen Nung and Bodhidharma are two characters in regional legends, credited with discovering tea, according to Buddhist texts.

Folklore tells us, Shen Nung, the Chinese emperor in 2732 BC, was boiling water when few leaves from branches being used as firewood fell into a vessel and gave a unique flavour to the water. Those were tea leaves!

Shen Nung (divine husbandman) laid down the basis for Chinese agriculture and was a renowned herbalist. Certain narratives suggest that he spoke after three days of his birth, walked after a week and was able to plough a field at the age of three!

Scrolls show that tea drinking existed in China in 6th century BCE, basically as medicine.

Bodhidharma was a Buddhist monk, born

Lord Macartney in Peking: How the English tried to capture China's tea trade

at Kanchipuramin, Tamil Nadu, in 520 AD. The story about him discovering tea is also quite interesting. He had travelled all the way to China to spread Buddhism. It is said that whilst meditating he fell asleep. Upset with himself and to prevent it from happening again, he cut off his eyelids. Where they fell, two tea plants grew. Buddhist lore says that this forms the traditional basis for Zen monks to drink tea to keep awake during meditation.

It was under the T'ang dynasty that this quintessential beverage became a highly sought-after commodity in the trading circles. So much so that it was extolled by the poets like Lu Yu and Lu T'ung in their compositions.

ChaKing, an ode to this magical shrub, was the very first monograph on tea in the world and was composed by Lu Yu. No wonder, tea merchants during that era considered him a patron saint.

Under the Song dynasty (960-1280 CE), the nuances of preparing that perfect cup, reached its heights. Special emphasis was laid on the quality of water, tea shrub, the accessories like utensils and potteries and this soon led the way for the fashionable tea contests amongst the upper strata of Chinese society of the time and the cultured elite.

The *Ta KuanCh'aLun*, written by Emperor Hui Tsung (1101-1125), became the tea connoisseur's bible. The book described the preparation of powdered green tea with a special cleft bamboo stick, special utensils used to whip tea into froth, had paeons dedicated to the virtues of this mystic brew that freed the mind from both physical and mental stress and helped attain instant nirvana.

Soon tea became a part of Chinese cuisine along with salt, rice and vinegar. It was emphasised that young maidens whose diet was devoid of strong spices, onions and garlic would be employed to handle the precious tea leaves.

Till the mid seventeenth century, Chinese tea was basically Green Tea. It was only with the increase in foreign trade that the plantation owners and merchants realised that they had to preserve the tea leaves for a longer period of time.

This they achieved by a special fermentation process and the resultant black tea had a stronger flavour, aroma quite distinct from the delicate green tea.

As time passed China's neighbours like Japan, South East Asian countries, Mongolia, Tibet amongst others picked up this tea-drinking habit. Overland routes carried the knowledge of tea to the Middle East. Tea and exquisite Chinese porcelain made its way to the western shore in the seventeenth century on the Dutch East India Company vessels.

The Chinese were intensely protective and controlled the cultivation of this shrub. They had the monopoly as the planet's only tea-producing country. The rising demand for tea in Europe prompted the Chinese to place poor quality tea in the market. They even started sending 'blue tea' which was nothing but green tea mixed with gypsum powder to satisfy the foreign demand in Europe and America.

Europe wanted tea under their control, especially the British, In 1793, the English sent a team headed by Lord George McCartney, their first ambassador to Peking.

The English thought they would be allowed to trade freely with the Chinese, but this did not happen. China was hesitant about trading with the west and took steps towards self-sufficiency and further isolation.

BURMA

Another legend suggests that King Alaungsithu (1111 – 1167) from Tawngpeng in Burma obtained tea seeds from a magical bird. He told his people that the seeds be planted near a local pagoda and that custodianship be given to the Palaung, a people who had their origins from a union between a Naga Princess and the Sun King. The tea plant was, indeed, held in high esteem.

TIBET

By ninth century, tea had been introduced to the Tibetans by the Chinese. The mountainous terrain and severe climate in this high-altitude region made tea cultivation impossible. So, tea started being imported from China via yak caravans. The tea leaf here is boiled for a good half an hour before straining the liquid. Tibetans add yak butter and salt to the tea and churn it. Probably this is done to replace the fat and salt which is lost by the mountainous dwellers. An interesting etiquette these highlanders follow is that no guests should leave without a cup of tea and also, the cup is kept refilled the moment it is drained.

JAPAN

At almost similar time, Japanese tourists in China were introduced to tea. A Buddhist monk, Saicho, a member of the Tendai sect was the first to bring tea plants to Japan from China, in the early ninth century. Tea spread as an accompaniment to spiritual exercises in the land. Monks would consume large bowls of Matcha, a powdered green tea rich in antioxidants and vitamins, in order to perform long hours of meditation without getting exhausted.

Japan's Precious Dew, also known as Gyokuro, is cultivated with utmost care and the process is quite unique. Few weeks before the harvest, just as the first buds appear, the entire plantation is covered with bamboo mats or dark canvas to prevent strong light coming in. The tiny leaves growing in semi darkness has higher chlorophyll and a lower tannin content, making it less bitter. This rare tea is harvested only once a year in late April or early May and is plucked according to the imperial method, only the tender bud and sometimes the first leaf. The powder form of this perfect tea is the subtle 'matcha tea' used in traditional tea ceremonies.

A very popular Japanese green tea, Sencha, is cultivated almost everywhere in the country, with a wide range of this tea being available at different price points. After the steaming process, the tea leaves are rolled and dried to remove humidity and give the leaves their characteristic needle shape. It was the Japanese Buddhist monk Baisao (master Matsuo Basho), around 1735 CE, who is credited with helping make sencha tea popular. He was of the opinion that tea can lead to spiritual enlightenment, a point which was emphasised in his poems.

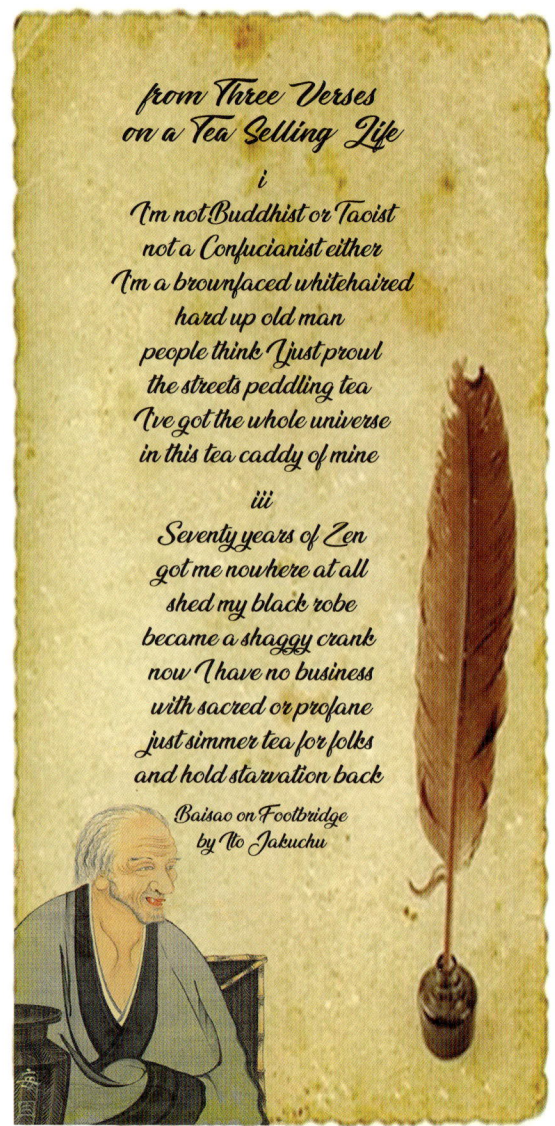

from Three Verses on a Tea Selling Life

i

I'm not Buddhist or Taoist
not a Confucianist either
I'm a brownfaced whitehaired
hard up old man
people think I just prowl
the streets peddling tea
I've got the whole universe
in this tea caddy of mine

iii

Seventy years of Zen
got me nowhere at all
shed my black robe
became a shaggy crank
now I have no business
with sacred or profane
just simmer tea for folks
and hold starvation back

Baisao on Footbridge by Ito Jakuchu

'Way of Tea' is all about the poetic beauty of Japanese spiritual thinking and beliefs. Believed to be one of the keystones of Japanese culture, the *chad* or the tea ceremony, is a classic embodiment of aestheticism and philosophy in perfect harmony.

The aristocrats (1338-1573) during that period began building 'tea cottages' for the tea ceremony, relaxing and watching the tea master as he went about preparing this exquisite brew.

Japanese tea gardens sculpt the terrain so beautifully that from a distance they resemble motionless waves of emerald green liquid.

The Japanese tea ceremony is a ritual of purity and simplicity, based on an ancient Zen Buddhism philosophy 'wabisabi' – that is learning to accept the natural ebb and flow of life cycle while embracing the imperfections that comes with it gracefully.

As Yasunari Kawabata has rightly said, 'A tea ceremony is a communion of feeling, when good friends come together at the right moment, under the best conditions.

TEA AND HAIKU

'Tea and poetry have an inextricable link. The mere process of drinking a cup of tea invites quiet contemplation which, in turn, provides the proper mental terroir for self-expression, like poetry. As a result, there's no dearth of tea-inspired poetry', writes Ryan MacMichael. Yet another expert tea blog says, 'poetry is the perfect companion for tea' and goes on to explain that the unique three-line poem format called Haiku is especially suited to tea as subject matter.

'Among the many names, is haiku writer Kobayashi Yatarō (1763-1828), known by his pen name Issa 一 茶. Issa literally means 'one (cup of) tea' and refers to the serenity of the Japanese tea tradition, but also to the emptiness of life, as can be observed in the disappearing froth on a cup of matcha tea', writes another blogger Nippaku. Issa wrote more than 20,000 haiku. His style is characterised by a simplicity and childish admiration for the outside world.

折ふしは鹿も立添茶つみ哉
orifushi wa shika mo tachisou cha tsumi kana
now and then the deer
stand close by…
tea pickers

朝茶のむ僧静也菊の花
asacha nomu sō shizukanari kiku no hana
drinking morning tea
the monk is peaceful
the chrysanthemum blooms (Basho)

RUSSIA

The land of Vodka discovered tea in the early seventeenth century when the Chinese gifted tea to Tsar Alexis. Tea gained popularity throughout the Russian empire by mid-nineteenth century, having been ferried from market to market even in far-flung villages.

Tea was only made accessible to everyone in Russia in the late 19th century. Before then, it was only consumed by the elite classes, and it is believed that the poor brewed herbal infusions in their samovars.

Russians drink both green as well as black tea without milk, often in glasses with metal handles and with a piece of sugar or some fruit jam which melts in the mouth while sipping on this strong bitter tea.

Russian Samovar

The Samovar, a large ornate urn is basically a combination of tea pot and brewing device. It is usually made of copper or bronze, and keeps water hot all day with its charcoal heated hot air system. The thee-tiered invention was created for the serving of tea. The bottom pot holds the steaming water, the second tier a robust black tea and the small pot at the top has herbal tea. Most northerly tea plantations in the world, the Krasnodar region, is in Russia. Despite having tea plantations, its tea output does not cover domestic demand. As a result, Russia imports tea from India and Sri Lanka to cater to the domestic consumption.

GERMANY

Tea was introduced to Germany in the seventeenth century by the Dutch. Soon the morning bowl of soup was replaced by a cup of tea. By nineteenth century, the Germans took this brew to another level by mixing rum, brandy, sugar, lemon and tea, christening it as 'Punch. By 1880, Indian and Sri Lankan black teas also started being imported to Germany. It was during the late nineteenth century that influenced by Japanese art and the German Art Nouveau, that tea became popular amongst the youth who found it more appealing than coffee, keeping with the sombre mood of the day. It was years later that the Germans' love of tea for the 'tea dances' came into vogue and it became fashionable for all generations to be on the floor of a ballroom of an upscale hotel, dance and enjoy a cup of tea.

THE ENGLISH TEA

Around 1610, the Dutch East India Company imported the first shipments of tea from China. The Dutch soon realised the lucrative power of this new merchandise and started getting back tea in humungous amount in each vessel returning from China. Within a century this exotic substance brought in from foreign shores became fashionable and elitist.

The British tea drinking habit was believed to have started around the seventeenth century when the King of England, Charles II married the Portuguese princess Catherine of Braganza. The new queen's supply of Chinese tea leaves evoked interest amongst the ladies and her habit of drinking tea in the afternoon became a fashionable trend to follow. Some historians claim that the word T E A comes from the words 'Transporte de ErvasAromaticas' – a cargo of fragrant herbs which was stamped on

Anna Russell, Duchess of Bedford

the tea crates which Catherine brought with her from Portugal.

Tea at that point in England was a very expensive commodity, basically because the English did not trade directly with China. Apart from that, the small quantities which the Dutch imported were sold at a very high premium.

Afternoon tea, a much-lauded English culinary tradition, was born in 19th century Britain when Anna Russell, the Duchess of Bedford, ordered tea and a light fare to her room between lunch and a late dinner.

It was quite different from high tea, which was born in the industrial era. Workers would have high tea served in the evening after work, with meats, eggs, cheese, bread and cake. High tea was more of a man's meal unlike afternoon tea which was served with delicate finger-foods and a lady's social diversion. It was, therefore, not surprising that the British immigrants in North America took 'tea-time' with them.

USA

The Dutch introduced tea to the USA in the early seventeenth century and it became fashionable amongst the elite class in Boston and Philadelphia to host tea parties and flaunt their exquisite silver teapots and porcelain tea wares. Tea slowly started percolating through the social layers and soon indulging and bonding over a cup of tea became associated with good manners and hospitality. As immigrants moved in from Europe and Asia, the upper classes in New England held on to their English custom of 'Tea'– It simply indicated the social status amongst the privileged class.

When the British found themselves financially strapped by the French and Indian wars, it imposed a 'tea tax' on its colonies, including in its American lands.

Violent protests by buyers followed as the tax rate reached an astronomical amount, more than doubling the initial cost of tea as it entered the American shores. This led to the famous 'Boston Tea Party' in 1773 .On 16 December, the inmates from Saint Andrew's masonic lodge in Boston entered three of the East India Company ships

The Destruction of Tea at Boston Harbor

Dartmouth, Beaver and Eleanor, dressed up as Native Americans and threw three hundred and forty tea chests into the harbour.

This was followed by another tea party in March 1774, when around 60 Bostonians boarded the ship Fortune and dumped nearly 30 chests of tea into the harbour.

The second incident didn't earn nearly as much notoriety as the first Boston Tea Party, but it did certainly led the way for other tea-dumping demonstrations in Maryland, New York and South Carolina. The series of events ultimately led to the America's Declaration of Independence in 1776.

Tea had indeed started a revolution. In around 1908, Thomas Sullivan, a New York based tea dealer, experimented with the idea of selling a single dose of tea in a tiny silk bag. This single serve tea bags met with huge popularity for the convenience it offered. It also had an impact on the way tea was prepared, leading the way for the production of inferior quality tea which could be crushed and packed in paper tea bags. The first modern tea bags were hand sewn fabric bags. Sullivan shipped his silk tea bags around the world. The first tea bag packing machine was invented in 1929 by Adolf Rambold for the German company Teekanne. The heat-sealed paper fiber tea bag was patented in 1930 by William Herman son. The now-common rectangular tea bag was not invented until 1944.

At the St Louis World Trade fair in 1904, a group of tea producers and dealers organised a tea pavilion and offered visitors a hot cup of tea. The heat and the sweltering summer condition proved to be a deterrent.

Richard Blechyden, a tea dealer had gone to the fair to introduce Americans to black tea from India which at that point still remained an unfamiliar commodity.

When he saw visitors shying away from drinking the hot beverage, he decided to add ice cubes in the glass, pour tea over it and offer to the attendees. This caught the attention of customers who queued up to try this new invention 'iced tea' Today , iced tea is consumed in the States often with lemon, sugar, sometimes even topping it up with rum.

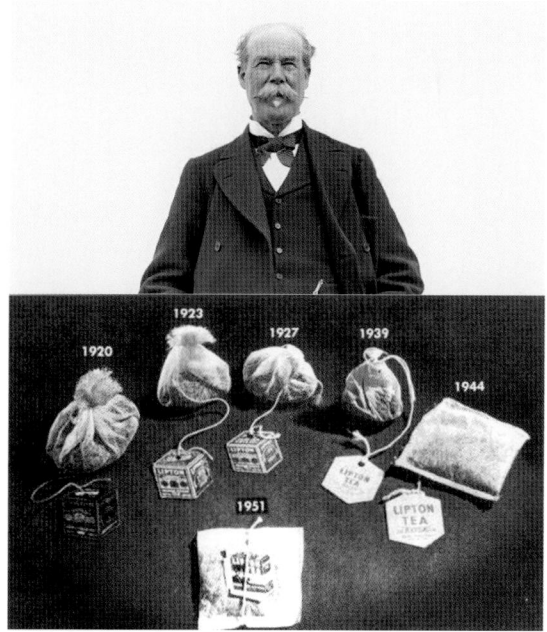

Thomas Sullivan and the tea bags he created

INDIA

Some records indicate that tea had been grown in India, in the native jungles of Assam way back in 750 BC. The Singphos, an ethnic group in the mountain regions of Arunachal Pradesh and Assam, had been consuming tea in medicinal forms. The wild tea shrubs in this mountainous area were about ten feet tall. These plants did not need any chemicals or fertilisers to nurture them. An interesting fact was that because of its heights, the Singphos used to ride on elephant back to pluck the tea leaves.

The way the leaves are processed are also different. The young tender tea leaves are plucked and dried in the sun. The tea leaves are then packed in the hollow of thick bamboo stalks. These tea laden stalks are then heavily smoked above a fire pit. After preserving the tea by smoking, it is then left to age for years.

The tea matures with age and the result is a delicious smoky tea, rich in antioxidants.

One can actually sense the subtle flavour of oolong and green tea in Phalap, sometimes also referred to as the 'pipe tea'. After a week of storing these bamboos, the processed tea hardens to take the shape of the tube. Small pieces are cut with a knife to brew a fresh cup of tea. When processed and brewed correctly, a cup of Singpho tea, which is had without milk or sugar, has a golden-orange hue. The leaves can be reused to brew two to three cups, the flavour keeps on getting better with each subsequent infusion.

With tea a big revenue earner, and the British unable to negotiate with China profitably in tea trade in the eighteenth century, how to get tea became a major concern of the East India Company.

pipe tea

The British then changed their strategy. Their colonies in India produced commodities which were highly valued in China. Whether it was cotton from Bengal or opium, the English traded products which found its way through all layers of the Chinese society.

The English started the opium war which helped them open Chinese ports, marking the end of Co-Hong monopoly.

Simultaneously, they embarked on a well-thought plan of growing tea in their Indian territories.

It was an Englishman named Robert Fortune who solved the enigma surrounding Chinese teas. He frequented the plantations which produced the finest teas under the guise of a Chinese trader. He managed to procure these precious tea seeds and in 1774, a shipload of tea seeds was brought from China to India and experimental planting was started in Calcutta. The traditional methods using these Chinese plants were, however, a failure.

The greatest impetus came from the 'discovery' of indigenous tea plants growing in the wilderness of Assam in the North Eastern part of India. The first European to have seen an Assamese tea bush was a Scot named Robert Bruce , who had made several trips to interior Assam in search of trade. He entered into an agreement with the Singpho Chief for supply of tea seeds and plants It soon became apparent that Robert Bruce's techniques produced excellent results.

It was only after the East India Company ended the monopoly of the Chinese trade in 1833 that the British government took firm steps towards the establishment of tea plantations in India.

This engraving shows the different stages in the process of making tea. Tea bushes are carefully pruned and plucked to maintain the correct density, encouraging new leaf-bearing shots

With Bruce having demonstrated the feasibility of cultivating and manufacturing tea in Assam, in 1839 the first company for growing and making tea in India, The Assam Company, was set up. This fuelled the dream that growing tea on Indian soil and creating plantations that could match those in China.

'The Calcutta' in 1838 sailed to London with twelve chests of Assamese teas. It was hailed as high point in the colonial rule – the British raj had produced its own tea. India's vast tea empire evolved under the British. They cultivated and consumed it in enormous amount during their rule in India.

Tea production in Sri Lanka

CEYLONE

In 1824, travellers like Maurice deWorms brought seeds of the tea plant from China to Ceylon. It was planted in the Royal Botanical Gardens, Peradeniya nurseries. The outcome was disappointing as the Chinese variety started stagnating.

Tea shrubs from Assam had reached the island of Sri Lanka (Ceylon in those days), a British colony in the Indian ocean in the 19th century. After the failure of the Chinese plants, planters here began to grow the ones brought in from the Indian shores of Assam in the island. In London, during the International Expositions in 1884 and 1886, the world got a glimpse of the teas from the British empire. However, the Ceylonese teas made a tremendous impact in 1893 in Chicago in the World Fair. By the end of the nineteenth century, tea as a word soon kindred with Ceylon and not China.

AN ACCOUNT
OF
THE MANUFACTURE
OF THE
BLACK TEA,
AS
NOW PRACTISED AT SUDDEYA
IN
UPPER ASSAM,
BY THE CHINAMEN SENT THITHER FOR THAT PURPOSE.
WITH
SOME OBSERVATIONS ON THE CULTURE OF THE PLANT
IN CHINA,
AND ITS GROWTH IN ASSAM.

By C. A. BRUCE,
Superintendant of Tea Culture.

CALCUTTA:

G. H. HUTTMANN, BENGAL MILITARY ORPHAN PRESS.

1838.

THE METHOD
OF MAKING
BLACK TEA.

In the first place the youngest and most tender leaves are gathered; but when there are many hands and a great quantity of leaves to be collected, the people employed nip off with the forefinger and thumb the fine end of the branch with about four leaves on, and sometimes even more, if they look tender. These are all brought to the place where they are to be converted into Tea; they are then put into a large, circular, open-worked bamboo basket, having a rim all round, two fingers broad (see fig 1). The leaves are thinly scattered in these baskets, and then placed in a framework of bamboo, in all appearance like the side of an indian hut without grass, resting on posts, 2 feet from the ground, with an angle of about 25° (fig. 2). The baskets with leaves are put in this frame to dry in the sun, and are pushed up and brought down by a long bamboo with a circular piece of wood at the end (fig. 3). The leaves are permitted to dry about two hours, being occasionally turned; but the time required for this process depends on the heat of the sun. When they begin to have a slightly withered appearance, they are taken down and brought into the house, where they are placed on a frame (fig. 4) to cool for half an hour.

A

---

* The Charles Bruce book pages reproduced here are from the collection of Larry Brown.

[2]

They are then put into smaller baskets of the same kind as the former, and placed on a stand (fig. 5). People are now employed to soften the leaves still more by gently clapping them between their hands, with their fingers and thumb extended, and tossing them up and letting them fall, for about five or ten minutes. They are then again put on the frame (fig. 4) during half an hour, and brought down and clapped with the hands as before. This is done three successive times, until the leaves become to the touch like soft leather; the beating and putting away being said to give the tea the black colour and bitter flavour. After this the Tea is put into hot cast-iron pans (fig. 6) which are fixed in a circular mud fire-place, so that the flame cannot ascend round the pan to incommode the operator. This pan is well heated by a straw or bamboo fire to a certain degree. About two pounds of the leaves are then put into each hot pan, and spread in such a manner that all the leaves may get the same degree of heat. They are every now and then briskly turned with the naked hand to prevent a leaf from being burnt. When the leaves become inconveniently hot to the hand, they are quickly taken out and delivered to another man with a close worked bamboo basket (fig. 7) ready to receive them. A few leaves that may have been left behind are smartly brushed out with a bamboo broom; all this time a brisk fire is kept up under the pan. After the pan has been used in this manner three or four times, a bucket of cold water is thrown in and a soft brickbat and bamboo broom used, to give it a good scouring out; the water is thrown out of the pan by the brush on one side, the pan itself being never taken off. The leaves all hot on the bamboo basket are laid on a table that has a narrow rim on its back, to

[3]

prevent these baskets from slipping off when pushed against it. The two pounds of hot leaves are now divided into two or three parcels, and distributed to as many men, who stand up to the table with the leaves right before them, and each placing his legs close together; the leaves are next collected into a ball, which he gently grasps in his left hand, with the thumb extended, the fingers close together, and the hand resting on the little finger. The right hand must be extended in the same manner as the left, but with the palm turned downwards, resting on the top of the ball of tea leaves. Both hands are now employed to roll and propel the ball along; the left hand pushing it on, and allowing it to revolve as it moves; the right hand also pushes it forward, resting on it with some force, and keeping it down to express the juice which the leaves contain. The art lies here in giving the ball a circular motion and permitting it to turn under and in the hand two or three whole revolutions, before the arms are extended to their full length, and drawing the ball of leaves quickly back without leaving a leaf behind, being rolled for about five minutes in this way (fig. 8). The ball of Tea leaves is from time to time gently and delicately opened with the fingers, lifted as high as the face, and then allowed to fall again. This is done two or three times, to separate the leaves; and afterwards the basket with the leaves is lifted up as often, and receives a circular shake to bring these towards the centre. The leaves are now taken back to the hot pans and spread out in them as before, being again turned with the naked hand, and when hot taken out and rolled; after which they are put into the drying basket (fig. 9) and spread on a sieve, which is in the centre of the basket, and the whole placed over a charcoal fire. The fire is very nicely regulated; there must not be the least smoke, and the charcoal should be well picked.

When the fire is lighted it is fanned until it gets a fine red glare and the smoke is all gone off; being every now and then stirred and the coals brought into the centre, so as to leave the outer edge low. When the leaves are put into the drying basket, they are gently separated by lifting them up with the fingers of both hands extended far apart and allowing them to fall down again; they are placed 3 or 4 inches deep on the sieve, leaving a passage in the centre for the hot air to pass. Before it is put over the fire the drying basket receives a smart slap with both hands in the act of lifting it up, which is done to shake down any leaves that might otherwise drop through the sieve, or to prevent them from falling into the fire and occasioning a smoke, which would affect and spoil the Tea This slap on the basket is invariably applied throughout the stages of the Tea manufacture. There is always a large basket underneath to receive the small leaves that fall, which are afterwards collected, dried and added to the other Tea; in no case are the baskets or sieves permitted to touch or remain on the ground, but always laid on a receiver with three legs (fig. 11). After the leaves have been half dried in the drying-basket, and while they are still soft, they are taken off the fire and put into large open-worked baskets (fig. 1) and then put on the shelf (fig. 4) in order that the Tea may improve in colour.

Next day the leaves are all sorted into large, middling, and small; sometimes there are four sorts. All these the Chinese informed me become so many different kinds of Teas; the smallest leaves they called Pha-ho, the 2d Pow-chong, the 3d Su-chong, and the 4th or the largest leaves, Toy-chong. After this assortment they are again put on the sieve in the drying basket (taking great care not to mix the sorts) and on the fire as on the preceding day; but now very little more than will cover the bottom of the sieve is put in at one time, the same care of the fire is taken as before, and the same precaution of tapping the drying basket every now and then. The Tea is taken off the fire with the nicest care for fear of any particle of the Tea falling into it. Whenever the drying basket is taken off, it is put on the receiver, (fig. 11) the sieve in the drying basket taken out, the Tea turned over, the sieve replaced, the tap given, and the basket placed again over the fire. As the Tea becomes crisp it is taken out and thrown into a large receiving basket, until all the quantity on hand has become alike dried and crisp; from which basket it is again removed into the drying basket, but now in much larger quantities. It is then piled up eight and ten inches high on the sieve in the drying basket, in the centre a small passage is left for the hot air to ascend, the fire that was before bright and clear, has now ashes thrown on it to deaden its effect, and the shakings that have been collected are put on the top of all, the tap is given and the basket with the greatest care is put over the fire. Another basket is placed over the whole to throw back any heat that may ascend. Now and then it is taken off and put on fig. 11, the hands with the fingers wide apart are run down the sides of the basket to the sieve, and the Tea gently turned over, the passage in the centre again made, &c. and the basket again placed on the fire. It is from time to time examined, and when the leaves have become so crisp that they break by the slightest pres-

[6]

sure of the fingers, it is taken off, when the Tea is ready. All the different kinds of leaves underwent the same operation. The Tea is now little by little put into boxes and first pressed down with the hands and then with the feet, (clean stockings having been previously put on.)

There is a small room inside of the Tea house, 7 cubits square and 5 high, having bamboos laid across on the top to support a net work of bamboo, and the sides of the room smeared with mud to exclude the air. When there is wet weather, and the leaves cannot be dried in the sun, they are laid out on the top of this room on the net work, on an iron pan, the same as is used to heat the leaves; some fire is put into it, either of grass or bamboo, so that the flame may ascend high, the pan is put on a square wooden frame (fig. 12) that has wooden rollers on its legs, and pushed round and round this little room by one man, while another feeds the fire, the leaves on the top being occasionally turned; when they are a little withered, the fire is taken away, and the leaves brought down and manufactured into Tea, in the same manner as if it had been dried in the sun. But this is not a good plan, and never had recourse to, if it can possibly be avoided.

A DIALOGUE BETWEEN MR. C. A. BRUCE AND THE CHINA BLACK-TEA MAKERS.

Does the China Tea plant grow mostly on the mountains of China or in the vallies? "About seven parts grow on the mountains and three in the vallies." Does the Tea plant grow amongst the snow? "Yes." Does not the snow kill or hurt the plants? "It hurts them very little, it may kill some of the old trees, but often new shoots come up from the old plants." To what

[7]

age does the Tea plant attain in your country? "Generally, about fifty years, but some only live ten." How do you plant the Tea seeds? "I dig a hole about four fingers deep and eight inches in diameter, and put as many seeds as I can hold in both hands into it, then cover it up." How long is it before the seedlings come up, and in what months do you put them into the ground? "We sow some in November and December, and some in January; when the rains set in they come up." When are the plants fit for plucking? "Sometimes in the third, and sometimes in the fourth year, according to the soil." How high are they in the third year? "From one to two cubits; a great deal depends on the soil." If you were not to pluck the leaves, would the plants grow higher? "To be sure they would; it is the constant plucking of the leaves that keeps the plants low." How many of the seeds that you sow come up in general? "If good seeds from ten to twenty." Do you allow them all to grow in the same place, or do you transplant them afterwards? "We allow them all to grow, and very seldom transplant; if we do, it is performed in the rains, and from four to six plants are put close together, so as to form a fine bush." At what distance is one Tea bush from another? "From three to four feet apart are small ridges of earth, eight inches to a foot high, a hollow space being left between to draw off the rain water; the bushes are at equal distances from each other, and in straight lines." Do you ever dig trenches to prevent the plants being washed away? "Yes, we are obliged to dig many; the shape and form of the trenches depend upon the ground and situation." What quantity of manufactured Tea do you think each Tea plant produces in one season? "This varies very much; some plants only produce two rupees weight, while others produce a pound and a half; but about a quarter of a pound, all round, I should think the first crop; the second crop a little less, and some people never take the third crop for fear of killing the trees." Do you always manufacture the Tea in China, in the same way as you have the Assam Tea? "The same." Do you know how to make Green Tea? "No." Do you ever put anything to the Tea to give it a flavour? "Never." Do you ever sow or plant in the shade, or have you any trees to shade the plants? "No, there are a few large trees here and there, but not for shade." If your plantations are on the side of mountains, they cannot have the sun all day? "True, in some plantations the plants are in the shade for nearly half the day; some China merchants that come to purchase Tea, pretend to know which is shady and which sunny by the smell, the sunny being preferred." Do the Tea plants cast all their leaves in the winter? "Great numbers fall, but the plants always retain some." Which do you think have the most juice when they are rolled, the leaves from the sunny tract, or those from the shady? "Those from the shady tract." Which require to be most dried in the sun? "The shady-tract leaves." Which of the two Teas do you think best? "That from the sunny tract." Which produce most leaves, those in the shade, or those plants that have been cut down, and afterwards permitted to grow up? "The latter twice as many." Which do you think produce most seeds? "Those in the sun." Do you ever in China plant from slips? "No." After you have made the Tea in China, how long is it before it is fit to drink? "About one year; if drank before that, it will taste unpleasantly and of the fire, and will affect the head." How long will Tea keep without being damaged? "If well secured from the air in boxes, it will keep good for three or four years." In which months do you commence plucking the leaves in China? "If the weather is warm and fine, and the season has not been a very cold one, the first crop commences in May, the second crop about forty-seven days after the first, and the third crop about the same time after the second, or forty-two days." When you roll the China leaves, do you think they contain more juice, or less, than the Assam ones? "The China leaves, I think, have more juice, and the leaves are much smaller." Is the soil of the China Tea the same as the Assam? "The same." How often do you weed your plantations? "Once in the rains and once in the cold weather."

The place these Chinamen speak of is called "Kong-see," on the mountains, about 40 days journey by water to Canton, and two days journey from the great Tea country "Mow-ee-san."

A few Observations on the Tea Plant of Assam.

The Tea plants in Assam have in general been found to grow, and to thrive best, near small rivers and pools of water, and in those places where, after heavy falls of rain, large quanties of water have accumulated, and in their struggle to get free, have cut out for themselves numerous small channels. The sort of land to which I allude will be perhaps letter explained by means of a diagram.

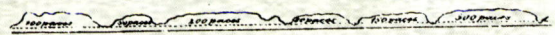

The dotted line shews the limit of the highest flooding. On the top of this land you must fancy a thick wood of all sorts and sizes of trees, and amongst these the Tea tree, struggling for existence; the ground here and there having a natural ditch cut by the rain water, which forms so many small Islands. The largest piece of ground that I have met with, I think was about 600 paces without a break. I also add a section of the little river Kahong, where the Tea plant abounds, exhibiting many small Islands, every one of which is covered with trees of various sizes, and the Tea among them; the land being never wholly inundated in the rains, though nearly so. This kind of land is called Coor-kah Mutty. I have never met with the Tea plants growing in the sun, but invariably under shade, in thick woods, or what we call tree-jungle, and only there, and in no other jungle whatever. It struggles for existence amongst so many other trees, that it becomes tall and slender, with most of its branches high up. The largest Tea tree I ever met with was 29 cubits high, and four spans round; very few I should say attain that size. I have taken great numbers of Tea plants from the jungles, brought them 4 to 8 days journey to my own house, and planted them in the sun, that is, without any shade; during the first six months the half of them died, at the end of the year about one quarter of what I had originally brought only lived; at the end of the 2d year there was still less; those that did live threw out leaves and blossoms, but the fruit never came to perfection. The plants I speak of were from one to three feet high; if they have grown any thing since they were transplanted, it has hardly been perceptible, either in height or thickness; many of them have had the advantage of a little shade from **the trees in my garden**, and those that had the most shade I find look healthier than those that had none, and they throw out more leaves. I have often read and heard of the China Tea plant growing no higher than three feet; their being planted in the sun and their leaves constantly gathered, I think accounts for it. A short time ago I requested and got permission from Government to try some experiments in my own way. About the middle of last March, I brought three or four thousand young plants from their native soil in the Muttuck country, about eight days journey, and planted them in the tree-jungles of this place, eight and ten close together, in deep shade. From 4 to 500 were planted in different places, some miles from each other; in the latter end of May I visited them and found them as fresh as if they had been in their native soil, throwing out fresh leaves. As these thrived so well, last June I brought from the same place 17,000 more young plants, and planted them in Coor-kah Mutty, about two miles from this place in deep shade; they are now throwing out new leaves and thriving as well as could be expected, although the soil here is nothing like that from whence they were taken—in which point alone the places differ. To shew how very hardy they are I may mention, that they were in the first instance plucked out by the roots by the village people who were sent to bring them from their native jungles, put upright into baskets without any earth, brought two days journey on men's backs, put upright into canoes, a little common earth only being thrown amongst their roots, and were from seven to twenty days before they reached me; and then they had to be carried half a day's journey to the intended new plantation, and were four and five days with only a little moist earth at their roots, before they were

[12]

finally put into the ground. And yet these plants are doing well; at least the greater part of them. I will give another instance of their hardiness. Last year the Government sent a deputation of three scientific gentlemen to examine the Assam Tea plant, Dr. Wallich, Mr. Griffith, and Mr. McClelland,—the two former Botanists, the latter a Geologist. Dr. Wallich who conducted the deputation, requested me to accompany them, being the only European who had ever visited the Tea tracts, as the different localities are called. One day after having seen some Tea in company with these gentlemen, and as we were returning, I was informed by some natives of another patch or tract of Tea that had been cut down. We went and examined it, and found the plants just coming up, about 6 inches high. On enquiry we were told that the villagers took the Tea plant to be so much jungle, and therefore nearly cut all of it down close to the ground, and set fire to the whole, and then planted paddy or rice on the spot. The crop of paddy had just been cut and brought in; when we saw the plants, the shoots were coming up from the roots and old stumps, thick and numerous. Some Tea plants I noticed had only been cut a foot, and some two to four feet from the ground; all these threw out numerous shoots and leaves an inch or two below where they had been cut. I afterwards converted this piece of ground into a Tea garden on account of the Government, and now it is one of the finest I have; where there was formerly one Tea plant, there are now upwards of a dozen, the new shoots from the old cuttings forming a fine bush, and shewing a great contrast to some of the original trees, which I have permitted to stand, with slender trunks and a few branches only at the top. This tract or garden has yielded

[13]

more Tea this season, than twelve times the same space of ground in the jungles would have done. I found that as the plants that had been cut down grew up again, the leaves acquired a yellowish tinge from their exposure to the sun, and were much thicker than those in the jungles; but this yellow tinge has worn off, and the leaves are now as green as those in the shade. As this tract answered so well by being cut down and set fire to, I tried the same experiment upon another tract close by, and it has come up to what I expected of it, eight to twelve new shoots having risen from the old stumps in the place of one. It is now a very fine Tea tract. Not knowing how this plan of cutting down might answer eventually, and how it might effect the plants, I took another tract in hand, allowed all the Tea plants to remain, but cut down all the other trees, large and small, that gave them shade, piled them up, and what I could not set fire to, I threw into the water courses. These Tea plants are doing well, but still each plant remains single, consequently has not many leaves, and is much in the same condition as when under shade. We have not had sufficient time to show what effect the sun may have on the leaves, and the Tea made from them. This tract has a curious appearance, the plants appearing hardly strong enough to support themselves now they are deprived of their friendly shade. I have some other tracts under experiment; some where I have permitted the jungle trees to grow, and only cleared away the brushwood and other small trees to admit the rays of the sun; others with very little shade. I have cut off branches of the Tea plants and laid them horizontally in the ground, with an inch or two of earth on them, and they have thrown out numerous shoots the whole length of

[14]

the branch; other branches were simply pushed into the earth, and they have grown; but this was all in the shade. I do not think they would answer so well in the sun.

I have the pleasure of furnishing a map which I have made of all the Tea tracts I have discovered. Since it was composed several more tracts have been discovered, which I have not had time to enter. It should be observed, that south from Suddeeah to the Debree river is generally termed Chyquah. South of Debree river is called the Muttuck country, as far the Burro Dehing river. South of the Burro Dehing, river is situated Rajah Purundah Sing's country. From the hill and river called Jowrah Poong, which is nearly at the source of the Debree river, to a place called Beesa, south of the above hill, on the Burro Dehing river, near the little river Juglow Pauney, is called the Singpho country, being all to the east of the above line. Now it will be perceived, that not a single Tea tract has been discovered north of the Debree river, and that they are all on the south side of it. The Muttuck country, which I have traversed most, appears to me to be one vast Tea country, and I feel confident that not one half of its Tea tracts have been yet discovered. The whole of the soil of the Muttuck country appears well adapted for Tea; I have taken particular notice of it, digging and examining it at every place where I have stopped. Great numbers of the Tea tracts have been cut down in sheer ignorance by the natives and converted into paddy fields. I know of three tracts, where the paddy had been collected, and the Tea plants had sprung up again; when these are neglected they all rise up into thick wood jungle. Several of these places have been pointed out to me by some of the old inhabitants. Almost every inhabitant

[15]

of the Muttuck country know now the Tea leaf, seeing how much we prize it, and getting little rewards from me when they bring in a branch from any new tract. There is plenty of Tea in Rajah Purundah's country, but he is too lazy to trouble himself about it; he is not even acquainted with those places laid down in my map. I have lately heard of a very extensive tract in his country, said to be as large as a dozen tracts put together. Several tracts are 800 paces long and nearly the same in breadth, and others only 100; but they have not all been properly examined, and may prove much larger. All these tracts can be enlarged almost to any extent from the numerous seedlings that are found amongst the Tea plants, from the great number of seeds that can be collected every year, and from the immense number of cuttings that may be planted. With respect to the seedlings, I have sown numerous seeds at Suddeeah in the sun; many have come up and appeared to thrive very well for the first year, but there was an insect, the Mole Cricket I think it is called, which used to nip off the young and tender leaves, and carry them into a hole under ground near the root of the plant; and I never succeeded in getting one plant to live. But last year I sowed some seeds in my garden under the shade of trees and bushes, they have come up and are thriving very well. The seeds I sowed in the sun last year, in the Muttuck country, and in their native soil in one of my Tea tracts, have also come up and are doing well. The Tea tracts in the Singpho country are much larger than those in the Muttuck. The Singphos have known and drank the Tea for many years, but they make it in a very different way from what the Chinese do. They pluck the young and tender leaves and dry them a little in the sun; some put them out into the dew and then again into the sun three successive days, others only after a little drying put them into hot pans, turn them about until quite hot, and then place them into the hollow of a bamboo, and drive the whole down with a stick, holding and turning the bamboo over the fire all the time, until it is full, then tie the end up with leaves, and hang the bamboo up in some smoky place in the hut; thus prepared the Tea will keep good for years. A good way further east they dig holes in the earth, line the sides with large leaves, boil the Tea leaves, throw away the decoction, put the leaves into the hole, which they cover over with leaves and earth, and then allow the whole to ferment; after which it is taken out, filled into bamboos, and in this manner prepared taken to market. These Singphos pretend to be great judges of Tea. All their country abounds with the plant, but they are very jealous and will give no information where it is to be found, like the Muttuck people. All the Singpho territories are overrun with wood jungle, and if only the under wood was cleared, they would make a noble Tea country. The soil is well adapted for the plant. Nearly three years ago I by accident left a few Singpho Tea plants, which I had carried away, on the banks of the New Dehing, three days journey from the place where I had got them; they were discovered by some Singpho friends of mine and stuck into the earth; and there they are now growing, as if they had never been transplanted, and notwithstanding they were put in the shade. The Singpho country is a fine one, but as long as that nation can get the Tea leaves from the jungles, they never will cultivate the plant; the country is thinly inhabited by a set of men, who are always fighting amongst themselves. The Tea is said to grow on the top of the Nagah Hills, marked in my map, South of Ningrew, on the banks of the Burro Dehing. All the Tea tracts laid down are in the vallies.

The above observations have been thrown together in a hurry, without much order. I therefore hope that allowances will be made for their imperfections. I may at some other time resume the subject if it is thought of any interest.

C. A. BRUCE,
Supt. of Tea Culture in Assam.

[18]

Section of the Kahong River, shewing the different channels the water had cut out for itself. The river is dry in the cold season, its banks are steep; all the little Islands are covered with Tea plants under shelter of the other trees; they are of various sizes, from 5 paces to 200, but near the bed of the river itself they are rather small. This kind of land is called *Coor-kah Mutty*.

EXPLANATION OF THE PLATES.

PLATE I.

Fig. 1. Dallah or large bamboo basket for drying the tea leaves in, with a rim all round; 2½ feet in diameter.

Fig. 2. Bamboo frame supporting the baskets with fresh gathered leaves drying in the sun; some of the baskets are represented as placed on the frame.

Fig. 3. Bamboo with a circular piece of wood at the end, used for pushing up, and bringing down the dallahs or baskets with leaves; the circular wood taking hold of the rim.

Fig. 4. Frame having three or more shelves made of bamboos placed lengthways, for holding the dallahs with leaves, after they have been removed from the sun.

Fig. 5. Stand on which the basket is placed, 2 feet 8 inches wide, and 2 feet 6 inches high.

Fig. 6. Cast-iron pan placed on a mud fire place, for heating the leaves; 2 feet 1 inch in diameter, and 7½ inches deep.

PLATE II.

Fig. 7. Close-worked basket, 2 feet 4 inches in diameter, with an edge all round, used for receiving the leaves from the pan, and for rolling them on, after it has been placed on the table.

Fig. 8. The left hand grasping the leaves about to be rolled, resting on the little finger; the extended right hand with the fingers close together, except the thumb, which is stretched out; ready to be placed on the leaves received from the left hand.

Figs. 9 & 10. Drying basket lined with paper on purpose to retain the heat better, and placed over a charcoal fire.

Fig. 11. Stand for a large circular basket, for receiving the shakings from the drying basket when placed on it, to remove the sieve and to turn the leaves during the process of drying.

Fig. 12. Stand with four legs each having a wooden roller, 2 feet 8 inches high and 1 foot 6 inches broad on each side. Fig. 12, b, represents this stand with the cast-iron pan on it.

Fig. 13. Basket used for various purposes, such as shaking and cleaning the leaves, carrying the dry tea, &c.

Fig. 14. The large circular basket, Fig. 7, on the stand Fig. 11, having on it the drying basket with the sieve fixed to the middle by means of small bamboo pegs.

---

* The illustrations of the plates as detailed here were missing from the original document but similar old manufacturing techniques were used by the early Cachar planters and the illustrations reproduced here are those as used by Samuel Cleland Davidson (Sirocco Founder) at his Burkhola T.E.

Old method of rolling the leaf

Old method of fermenting the leaf

Old Method of drying the leaf

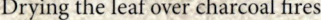

Drying the leaf over charcoal fires

Hand Sorting of the Finished tea

Gratitude

I feel incredibly lucky that I got to work with such wonderful and talented experts whose illuminating articles enrich the leaves of this book. Sanjay Khosla, Piyush Pandey, Ashok Mittal, Alyona and Sanjeev Kapoor, Chandrajit Banerjee, Suhel Seth, Larry Brown, Rinku Madan, Arnab Banerjee, Sangeeta Kichlu, Neera Sareen and Tapasya Mundhra, thank you for trusting me.

I would also like to thank my publisher Renu Kaul Verma, editor Papri Sri Raman, designer Somesh Kumar Mishra and the entire team at Vitasta Publishing for helping me negotiate the intricate path of this Coffeetable book. The design, the visualization couldn't have been done without them. Avanish Trivedi, thank you for the painting you shared.

I acknowledge all sources like Wikipedia, Unsplash, Cooking From Heart, Wallpaper Cave, tarladalal.com, Chits Kitchen, everydayeileen.com, Chai Time Feature Credit Chefyash, Wallpapersafari, The biote, Tea floor, silencesings.blogspot.com, koi-hai.com, Teafields.co.uk, Tibet Travel, Leavla, Colombo Telegraph, antareshistoria.com, Life in Chandigarh, The afternoon tea club and Pipes Magazine for pictures used in the book.